A FRIGATE OF
KING GEORGE

For Margaret

A FRIGATE OF KING GEORGE

Life and Duty on a British Man-of-War 1807–1829

BRIAN VALE

I.B.Tauris *Publishers*
LONDON ● NEW YORK

Published in 2001 by I.B.Tauris & Co. Ltd
6 Salem Road, London W2 4BU
175 Fifth Avenue, New York, NY 10010
www.ibtauris.com

In the United States of America and Canada distributed by
St Martin's Press, 175 Fifth Avenue, New York, NY 10010

ISBN 1-86064-654-9

A full CIP record for this book is available from the British Library
A full CIP record for this book is available from the Library of Congress

Library of Congress catalog card: available

Typeset in Garamond by A. & D. Worthington, Newmarket
Printed and bound in Great Britain by MPG Books Ltd, Bodmin

CONTENTS

ILLUSTRATIONS

PLATES

PREFACE

This book is about His Majesty's Ship *Doris*. She was in fact the second Royal Navy frigate to bear that name in the Napoleonic Wars. The first had been constructed at Gravesend in 1795, and was one of a wave of powerful 36-gun ships modelled on the lines of *Flora* and *Perseverance*, which were beginning to dominate the scene during the 1780s. All bore names with impeccable classical origins even if they sound odd to the modern ear – like *Doris*, *Flora*, *Phoebe*, *Leda*, *Fortunee* and *Iphigenia*. Unfortunately the original *Doris* was wrecked in Quiberon Bay during January 1805, but its disappearance left a blank in the Navy List that enabled the Admiralty to sort out the confusion that distance and time lags had caused over the name of a new Indian-built frigate.

This book tells the story of the second *Doris* from the time she was constructed in Bombay in 1807 to the moment she was sold and broken up in Valparaiso in 1829. But it concentrates on one four-year commission between 1821 and 1824 when she was taken out of reserve in the bleak mudflats off Sheerness and sent to the South America station. There she formed part of the squadron which, under the command of Nelson's old Flag Captain Sir Thomas Hardy, was safeguarding British political and commercial interests amid the confusing struggles for independence that followed the Napoleonic Wars. The substantial trade that Britain had developed in the region since 1808 came under immediate threat, and both local British commercial communities and merchant ships found themselves uncomfortably in the front line between the rival factions. It was the Navy that had to provide protection. There was the normal function of shipping home the huge profits of British trade in silver and bullion. There were blockades to contend with as both the royalist and patriot navies –

the latter generally commanded and manned by British sailors under the ubiquitous Lord Cochrane – attempted to control the seas and cut off the flow of supplies to their enemies. And there were political challenges as well. British diplomats were only present in Brazil, so in Spanish America naval officers found themselves acting as floating consuls, intervening to protect British communities against forced loans or unfair trading restrictions, providing situation reports to the Foreign Office, and delicately attempting to maintain British neutrality in a series of conflicts between old political allies and new commercial partners. The operations of *Doris* and of other ships of the squadron as they ceaselessly patrolled the South Atlantic and the Pacific provide an illuminating insight into the peacetime duties performed by the Navy and of the successes it achieved.

But at this time, officers and men of the Royal Navy were faced with challenges of a more personal nature. The years that followed the Napoleonic Wars saw the size of the Royal Navy decline sharply. Between 1814 and 1820, the number of British ships in commission fell from 713 to 134, and the numbers of men from 140,000 to a mere 23,000. By 1820, 90 per cent of the 5264 officers on the Navy List were unemployed and living on half pay. And there were many more midshipmen, master's mates and warrant officers without even this compensation. The effect of this slump on the career prospects of officers in terms of appointments, promotions and retirement, or the lack of them, has been examined in general terms in a number of books. So has the impact of such things as 'interest' – or string pulling by the aristocracy and the politically influential – to improve an officer's prospects. There have, however, been few studies of how these affected one identified group of men over a particular period of time. In the pages that follow, I have tried to do this in relation to the South America Squadron in general and the *Doris* in particular.

Naval fiction continues to be a popular and absorbing form of literature. The naval novels of C.S. Forester, Patrick O'Brian, Alexander Kent, Richard Woodman and others are widely read and appreciated. Yet each writer has a different vision of life on a wooden warship. What was it really like? This book tries to answer the question in relation to His Majesty's Ship *Doris*. Drawing on official letters, logs, muster rolls, pay books, private letters and journals, it attempts to describe the everyday lives, duties and preoccupations of the officers and men who were on board the frigate during its four-year commission. It looks at the everyday routines of naval life in terms of shipboard organization, maintenance, recruitment, seamanship and supply, and examines the factors that were of particular importance to the lives of the men, such as food, drink, health, discipline and flogging. Finally it tries to provide insights into the lives of the ship's company when they were not on duty – crossing the line ceremonies, dances on board and parties in port, shore excursions, tourism, playacting, botanizing, 'hunting, shooting and fishing'. The result is a detailed account of real life and duty in one ship of the Royal Navy at the beginning of the nineteenth century during the reigns of King George III and IV. I leave it to readers to decide which of their favourite naval novelists is closest to the truth.

I would like to express my thanks to the Director and staff of the Public Record Office, Kew, for the efficient supply of the official documents on which this work is based, and to the Director and staff of the National Maritime Museum, Greenwich, for access to their records, to their picture and print collections, and for permission to use so many of them in the text.

Brian Vale
Greenwich

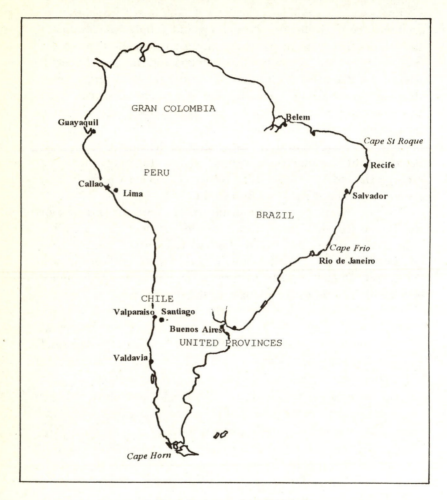

1 South America 1821-9

CHAPTER 1

EARLY DAYS: BOMBAY TO
SHEERNESS – 1807 TO 1821

The story of the *Doris* begins with Admiral the Earl of St Vincent. In 1801 the government of William Pitt was sacked by King George III and was replaced by an administration of mediocrities led by Henry Addington. The only man of stature in the new cabinet was St Vincent who became First Lord of the Admiralty with a programme that included a purge of dockyard corruption and an attack on what he saw as sharp practice by the contractors who supplied the Navy's timber. But the head-on tactics that had served the stern, gouty old Admiral so well against the Spanish and French were inadequate to this task. All he did was to stir up a hornet's nest. Faced with the onslaught, the wood merchants turned to other customers, and the Navy – already worried about diminishing supplies of oak – found itself facing a serious shortage of timber. The Admiralty began to seek supplies elsewhere.

An obvious place to look was India, and particularly the East India Company's well-established dockyard in Bombay. Sited on a fringe of sweltering marshy islands between the Western Ghat Mountains and the deep blue Arabian Sea, Bombay was already one of the Royal Navy's principal bases in the East. It boasted a fort, an arsenal and a hospital, and the adjacent Company dockyard had all the facilities needed for the construction and repair of warships – a smithy, a rope walk, mast ponds, dry docks and storehouses. Under the direction of the Wadias, a famous family of Parsee master builders, Bombay had become the Company's major centre for shipbuilding in the East, and specialized in the use of teak. The oils contained in this timber not only frustrated

1

the appetites of the boring insects that plagued wooden warships, but seasoned quickly to produce a durable wood particularly suitable for service in tropical waters. They also protected metal against corrosion with the result that Bombay ships were fastened with iron nails rather than wooden ones as in Europe. The main disadvantages of teak as a material for warship construction were that its hardness tended to blunt the shipwrights' tools and, if the wood splintered in action, the resulting wounds tended to turn septic.

In April 1802 St Vincent wrote to the East India Company, floating the idea that Bombay dockyard should begin an annual programme of building one frigate and one 74-gun ship-of-the line for the Royal Navy's use.[1] The expansion of the yard to cope with this order required the extension of its dry dock facilities and a great deal of investment, but the Company agreed, quoting a basic price of £21,377 for a frigate and £38,412 for a two-decker, slightly more than the cost of building in Britain.[2] The terms of the final deal were much to the advantage of the Company, a fact which its local agents did not hesitate to exploit. The Admiralty had to commit itself to paying the basic building cost plus 20 per cent, to provide all the tools, ironwork and copper that were needed, and to pay for the hire of the dry dock.[3] The following year the Admiralty sent out the plans so that preparations could begin. In July 1803 Franjee Maneckjee Wadia started work on the first of these vessels, a 36-gun frigate of 930 tons, based on a draft of the *Perseverance* class as adapted from the standard lines by Sir Edward Hunt. As noted triumphantly in the *Asiatic Annual Register*, the ship – suitably illuminated and initially called the *Pitt* – was launched at midnight on 17 January 1805, to the blare of a military band, the acclamation of the spectators and a salute from a gun battery.[4]

By this time William Pitt was back in power. St Vincent had left the Admiralty and had been replaced as First Lord by Henry Dundas, First Viscount Melville. Melville, a lawyer and politician with a rough manner and a strong Scots accent, was an ardent supporter of Pitt, and was effectively his party manager north of the border. In this role he had built up such a potent and extensive network of family and political patronage that he had become the most powerful man in Scotland. Melville promptly reversed most of St Vincent's policies, but his India initiative remained intact. The new First Lord had served for some time on the India Board of Control and was not only interested in the Sub-Continent, but claimed to have thought up the idea of building Royal Navy ships in Bombay in the first place.

His Scots patronage network also extended itself into the region and the place was filled with Campbells, Farquars, Macleods and Mackenzies. The Marine Superintendent at Bombay was a member of the extensive Dundas clan; and so was Captain George Dundas, the naval officer who was sent out in 1808 to act as Naval Commissioner to supervise the building programme. Serving as a naval officer in the American War, George Dundas had been made a lieutenant in 1783 and had then left for a job in the Revenue Service. In spite of this move into relative obscurity, his connections secured his promotion to Post Captain only two years later. Since promotion to admiral was awarded by seniority on the Captain's List, Dundas thus took his place on a moving staircase, which would eventually lead to flag rank. It also secured him two appointments in command of the 74-gun *Elephant* on the West Indies station during the Napoleonic Wars.

With Melville's backing, the Navy's construction programme in Bombay went on apace. Spectators who were more accustomed to the grime of European shipyards were amazed by the spectacle of neat white-clad shipwrights and artisans swarming over the vessels as they grew in the slips. *Pitt* was taken over and commissioned by the veteran Captain James Vashon, who was transferred with his crew from the *Fox* when she was laid up in Bombay for repairs. The idea that a ship named after the Prime Minister could only be made operational with the help of another bearing the name of the Leader of the Opposition caused much hilarity at the time. For the next 12 months *Pitt* formed part of the detachment that was blockading Mauritius, returning with her crew decimated by scurvy and James Vashon ailing.[5] The frigate then acquired a new captain in the shape of Walter Bathhurst, and spent the following year on convoy duty with Sir Edward Pellew's squadron in the East

Indies.[6] In September 1807 she acquired a new name, for the Admiralty had decided to rename her *Salsette*, and returned to Portsmouth for a refit. *Salsette* then formed part of the expedition that Sir James Saumarez took to the Baltic in March 1808, serving subsequently in the North Sea with the ill-fated Walcheran expedition and in the Mediterranean, before ending the war as she had begun it in the East.[7]

Meanwhile the Bombay construction programme continued and, in April 1806, work began on a second frigate, built to the same plans as the *Pitt*. Less than a year later, the new ship was launched into the blue waters of Bombay harbour on 24 March 1807 by Sir Edward Pellew himself. Her total cost was £39,774.[8] Unfortunately, owing to a mistake, made worse by the six-month time lapse between London and Bombay, she too was called *Salsette*. Hearing from the Admiralty in late 1805 that the new frigate was to be called *Salsette* and that Captain George Hardinge was on his way from England to take command, Pellew assumed they were referring to the vessel that was about to be built.[9] Only later was it revealed that they meant the *Pitt*.[10] *Pitt* was eventually renamed *Salsette* in September 1807, but Captain Hardinge and his officers became involved in Sir Home Popham's capture of the Cape of Good Hope on the way out, arrived late, and were appointed to the *San Fiorenzo*, in command of which Hardinge was tragically killed during the capture of the French frigate *Piédmontaise*. Meanwhile the new frigate had been launched also as *Salsette* and was given to Pellew's Flag Captain Christopher Cole. It took Cole five months to fit her out and raise a crew, but she was at sea by August. But the Navy now had two identical ships with the same name – a fact that confused the publishers of Steel's monthly *Navy List* at the time and has puzzled naval historians ever since. Becoming aware of the problem, the Admiralty decided to re-christen *Salsette* (2) and in September 1807 she became *Pitt* – a change which only added to the confusion. Finally, in March 1808, the frigate's name was changed again to the form she was to keep for the rest of her career. She became His Majesty's Ship *Doris*.

Meanwhile the extension of the Bombay dry dock had been

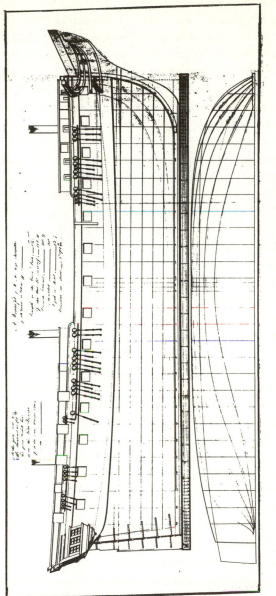

2 The lines to which *Salsette/Doris* wa built
National Maritime Museum London

completed, and work began on the construction of the first two-decked 74-gun ship, the *Minden*. The India building programme was continued with equal enthusiasm by Lord Melville's son, the second Viscount, when he began a historic 18-year stint as First Lord in 1812, and the dockyard – now under the direction of Jamsetjee Bomanjee – went on to produce a series of vessels that were to be as famous for their sailing qualities as their longevity – ships like *Cornwallis*, *Wellesley*, *Melville*, *Ganges* and *Asia*. The Admiralty presented Jamsetjee with a piece of handsome plate as a token of thanks and admiration.

Doris spent the next five years in the East Indies. Under the command of Captain William Lye, she formed part of the force with which Vice Admiral Albemarle Bertie captured Mauritius in 1810, and she was with Rear Admiral Robert Stopford when he took Java in 1811. It was Lye who brought her back to Plymouth at the end of 1812 for a refit. But in March 1813 *Doris* and her new Captain Robert O'Brien were heading east again in charge of a convoy of East India Company ships bound for India and China. By another coincidence, her fellow convoy escort was *Salsette*, now commanded by Captain John Bowen. Once round the Cape of Good Hope, Bowen was to see eight merchantmen as far as Madras, while O'Brien continued with the other five to Canton.[11] *Doris* then remained on trade protection duties in the South China Sea. There was one untoward event when she went aground on an uncharted rock, ripped off her false keel and severely damaged the timbers round her stem. The dockyard facilities in the port of Macao were limited, but O'Brien had the ship hauled on to her side and was able to carry out repairs with the help of the Portuguese governor after the payment of heavy bribes to the Chinese authorities.[12] That done, *Doris* returned to her task of commerce protection, watching out for the USS *Essex*, which was known to be at large in the Pacific, and hunting American privateers. She picked up a few prizes, but *Essex* never appeared and her pursuit of privateers was uniformly unsuccessful. The Americans were too fast and handy, and the frigate's attempts at capture were frustrated by maddening calms or by sudden squalls that prevented attacks by boats.[13]

HMS *Doris* was an example of the most common class of frigate. Ship-rigged with square sails on three masts, she measured 137 feet from stem to stern, was 38 feet wide and 14 feet deep in the hold. She had a displacement of 870 tons, was ballasted with 40 tons of shingle and 150 tons of pig iron packed tightly in the hold around the lower timbers of her frame, and drew 19 feet when fully loaded. Like all frigates, *Doris* had a single continuous gun deck stretching the whole length of the ship. Above that was the quarterdeck, which occupied the area behind the mainmast, and the fore deck, which filled the forward part of the ship. Between them was an open space called the waist, bounded on each side by wide gangways that linked the two. The gun deck's principal purpose was to carry artillery, but it had other uses as well. Beneath the fore deck was the forecastle, the location of the galley with its stove and cooker. And under the after part of the quarterdeck, sealed off from the rest by a partition, lay the captain's accommodation. This consisted of three units – a great cabin stretching across the full width of the ship and illuminated by the frigate's stern windows and, forward of that, a sleeping area and a fore cabin, also called the coach, divided by a partition. Below that lay the lower deck, also continuous and nicknamed the 'berth deck' since it was where the rest of the ship's company were accommodated. The seamen slung their hammocks in the foreward part. The Royal Marines occupied the centre. The after part was for the officers. The midshipmen and mates berthed and had their mess in the area around the main mast and hatchway. And from there to the stern lay the quarters of the commissioned and warrant officers – a long wardroom in the centre where they socialized, and rows of small flimsy cabins built against the sides of the ship where they slept and worked. The lower deck lay below the waterline and could only receive natural light and air via the hatchways, but it had the advantage that the cabin partitions and personal effects of the occupants – unlike those of the captain – did not have to be swept away when the frigate went into action.

The rest of the ship was devoted to stores. Below the lower deck was the orlop – three great platforms with open spaces between to facilitate stowage. In the forward area was the sailroom

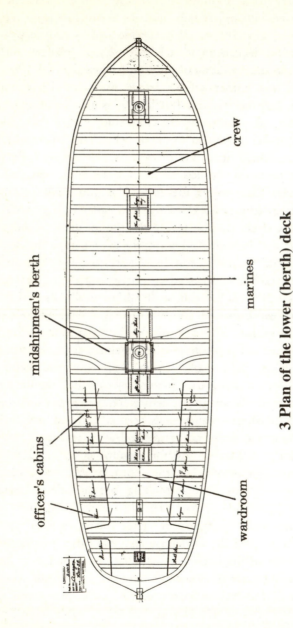

**3 Plan of the lower (berth) deck
National Maritime Museum London**

and the stores for boatswain's, carpenter's and gunner's material –
paint, pitch, wood, rope, tallow and so on. In the centre was the
drainable tier where the hemp anchor cables were coiled and
stored when not in use. And aft, in the driest part of the ship, lay
the bread room where biscuit and flour were stored in canvas
bags. Finally, at the lowest level, was the hold. This contained the
wooden leaguers and (after 1814) iron tanks that held the ship's
water supply and, wedged on the ballast against the ship's lower
timbers, hundreds of barrels – puncheons of beef and pork, butts
of wine and beer, hogsheads of vinegar and oatmeal, casks of
cheeses and oatmeal. In the centre were lockers for shot and
sealed magazines for gunpowder and, in the forward section, space
for the storage of firewood and barrel staves.

For much of her career *Doris* was classified as a '36-gun fifth-
rate' frigate although she actually carried 42 guns. These were
made up of a battery of 26 18-pounders on carriages stretching in
two rows to port and starboard along the gun deck; 12 32-pounder
carronades on the quarterdeck; and two carronades plus two long
9-pounder 'chase' guns on the forecastle. These were the most
accurate long-range weapons in the Navy's arsenal and, as their
name implies, were used for firing ahead when the frigate was
chasing an enemy. The original ships of this class had carried ten
rather than 16 guns on the two upper decks – all 9-pounders – but
the development in the 1780s of the carronade or 'smasher', a
shorter-range, heavier-calibre but lighter-weight weapon, changed
all that. The 9-pounder gun (classified, like all artillery, according
to the weight of the ball it fired) weighed over 25 cwt, was eight
feet in length, and needed a seven-man crew. The 32-pounder
carronade, as well as firing an infinitely more devastating shot, was
four feet long, weighed only 17 cwt, was mounted on a traversing
slide, and required only five men. Thus the Navy was happy to
replace eight of the upper deck long guns with 14 carronades
without affecting the vessel's stability, even though it made
nonsense of the rating system. The anomaly was only corrected
when there was a reclassification in 1817, and *Doris* was listed
more accurately as a 42-gun frigate.

Like all ships of her class, *Doris* carried five boats, all supplied

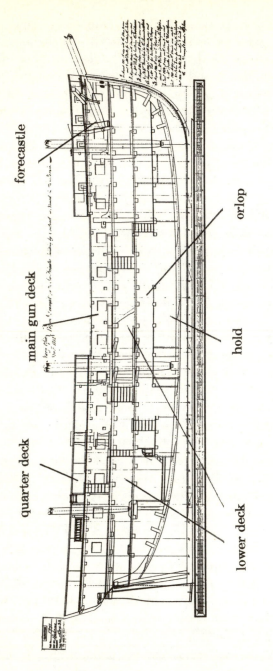

forecastle

main gun deck

quarter deck

lower deck

orlop

hold

4 Profile showing interior arrangements
National Maritime Museum London

with gear for sailing as well as oars. There was the launch, a large 26-foot working boat for harbour duties and carrying stores, a 32-foot pinnace and three smart cutters, two 24 and one 20 feet long. The last were used for lighter work including ceremonial visits by the captain and boat actions in time of war. When at sea, the pinnace and launch were carried in the waist; the cutters in davits each side of the quarterdeck.

In terms of performance, trials at Sheerness showed *Doris* to be 'strong, tight' and seaworthy, and found almost every aspect of her performance to be 'very good', whether riding at her anchors, wearing, standing under sail or stowing provisions. Half of her water supply – that is, 64 tons – was carried in iron tanks, which had proved to be more effective in keeping it fresh than wooden casks. Like other frigates her fighting qualities were enhanced by having main deck gun ports that were well clear of the water. Whereas, for example, the bottom sills on a ship-of-the-line were only six feet above the waves, in *Doris* the clearance was nine feet. She was also fast. With reefed topsails she could make nine knots, while under full sail she could cream along at 12 knots.[14] Bombay dockyard had done a good job.

With the coming of peace, *Doris* returned to England early in 1816 and was put in 'ordinary', that is in reserve. Her masts were taken out, her guns, stores and much of her ballast were removed, and her upper deck was temporarily roofed over to keep out the weather. Reduced to little more than a hulk, *Doris* was left in the charge of a handful of warrant officers and moored with other demobilized ships off Sheerness where the Medway meets the Thames estuary, the grey mudflats providing a gloomy contrast to the blue tropical waters in which most of her career had been spent. Only one major alteration was made during this period. In 1819 her 'waist' – that is, the gap between her quarterdeck and forecastle – was planked over, giving her a second continuous 'spar' gun deck after the fashion of the ships of the United States Navy encountered during the American War of 1812–14.[15] Apart from this change, *Doris* swung unmolested at her moorings, waiting until some national need would cause her to be recommissioned. In 1821 the call came. She was suddenly posted to the

Royal Navy squadron that was watching over British political and commercial interests in South America amid the revolutionary turmoil that followed the Napoleonic Wars.

CHAPTER 2

TURMOIL AND LIBERATION
IN LATIN AMERICA

The Napoleonic Wars had a devastating effect on the Spanish Empire in the Americas. In 1808 Napoleon invaded Spain, abducted the King, put his brother Joseph on the throne, and occupied the country. The result was a maelstrom of war and revolution. The usurper Joseph was roundly rejected by the Spaniards, and with the royal government headless, it was decided that elected juntas should be established at home and overseas to rule – temporarily it was hoped – in the name of the absent Ferdinand VII. But the King was not restored until 1815, and by this time the local American elites and military strong men had acquired a taste for self rule and for the economic benefits that freedom from the old trading restrictions had brought. They were not only determined to prevent the clock being put back, but were vigorously pushing it forward.

The reaction of the various South American provinces to the French occupation varied. In Peru the Viceroy refused to have any truck with the juntas and continued to rule in the King's name, but elsewhere the old regime was superseded and the move to autonomy began. Eventually, in the north, Simon Bolivar took dictatorial powers, overcame the royalists in Venezuela and Colombia and in 1814 established the Republic of New Granada. In the south the River Plate Provinces took the lead. Emboldened by its success in repelling the British invasion of 1806–7, the radical junta of Buenos Aires seized power, overthrew the Viceroy, and led an armed rebellion in the River Plate that eventually ejected the last royal representative from Montevideo. In 1813 an independent republic was proclaimed. The new regime promptly began sending liberating armies to Paraguay and Upper Peru, northwards through the Uruguay–Paraguay river systems, which provided the back door to the interior of the continent.

Spanish America was in turmoil, but in Brazil things were different. There the impact of Napoleon had produced an entirely different result. In 1807 the timid and irresolute Prince Regent, Dom João, had been persuaded to frustrate the French invasion of Portugal by fleeing to Rio de Janeiro with his Court, the whole apparatus of government and the entire contents of the treasury. Although relocated, the royal administration had therefore continued without disruption, and any vestigial colonial resentment in Brazil had been overcome by its new importance as the centre of the Portuguese Empire.

Meanwhile, back in Spain, Ferdinand VII, called – in spite of his cruel and twisted personality – 'El Deseado', that is 'the desired one', was restored to power in 1815. On a wave of patriotic enthusiasm, his government tried to roll back the revolutionary tide. A Spanish army under General Morillo reoccupied New Granada and forced Bolivar and his supporters to flee. Further south the royalist authorities roundly defeated three separate attacks by Buenos Aires on Upper Peru. Then the Portuguese marched into the Banda Oriental – ostensibly on behalf of Ferdinand VII, but in reality to realize their historic ambition of extending the frontiers of Brazil to the River Plate. And in the new republics themselves, there were bitter struggles for power. Revolutionary confidence began to wane and, seeing the realities of European power politics and the continuing prestige of monarchies, many radicals began to favour the idea that the newly independent South American states should be ruled by minor European royals. Spain, of course, had no such desire, and began to assemble a huge expeditionary force in Cadiz aimed at total reconquest.

The tide seemed to be turning, but not for long. In 1817 Bolivar was back to challenge the gains made by General Morillo. And in the River Plate, a fourth expedition was being mounted under the command of General José de San Martin. But this time, instead of going north, he headed west across the high peaks of the Andes, surprised and defeated the royalists at Chacabuco and proclaimed the independence of Chile. A second defeat at Maipú in 1818 put an end to any Spanish hopes of regaining control, and a new independent republic was formed under the dictatorship of Bernardo O'Higgins, the illegitimate British-educated son of an Irishman who had risen high in the Spanish royal service in South America.

While Bolivar prepared to advance southwards, San Martin paused in Chile to gather strength before leading his army north along the coast to attack the royalist fortress of Peru. However, military operations in the narrow strip between the Andes and the Pacific introduced a new dimension into the conflict – sea power. While the Spanish Navy commanded the waters of the Pacific no successful advance northwards was feasible. The Chileans therefore turned their energies to the creation of a navy. Men were recruited, officers were enlisted and merchantmen were converted into warships. Two brigs and a schooner were bought locally, and two new corvettes were ordered from the USA, although shortages of money meant that only one was eventually purchased. Soon unemployed British and American naval officers were flocking to Valparaiso to offer their services, more often than not bringing with them fully armed and manned warships to sell to the republican authorities. In this way the Chileans acquired and armed two East Indiamen, *Cumberland* and *Windham*, the former British sloop HMS *Hecate*, and an American brig called *Columbia*. These were renamed respectively *San Martin*, *Lautero*, *Galvarino* and *Araucano*.[1]

By 1818 the Chilean Navy boasted eight sizeable vessels, and added two more the following year when the Spanish warships *Maria Isabel* and *Potrillo* were captured. By then Chile's maritime forces comprised three frigates, two corvettes, four brigs, a schooner and numerous small fry. Recruitment had also gone well, and the new Chilean Navy now comprised 1600 sailors, 400 marines and 40 sea officers.[2] Although commanded by an Englishman, Major Miller, the marines were entirely Chileno, but two-thirds of the seamen and almost all the officers were British or

North American. Their numbers included at least nine officers with Royal Navy experience – Martin Guise and Robert Forster who had been commanders; J.T. Spry, T. Sackville Crosbie, Thomas Carter, lieutenants; and Robert Casey, Henry Freeman, Robert Simpson and Henry Cobbett – nephew of William Cobbett the radical pamphleteer – midshipmen. All in all, the Chilean Government had done well, but the masterstroke was its choice of commander-in-chief, no less a person that Lord Thomas Cochrane.

Lord Cochrane, a tall red-headed Scotsman and heir to the Earl of Dundonald, had been one of the Royal Navy's most outstanding frigate captains during the Napoleonic Wars. He had first shown his ingenuity and daring in 1800, when, in command of a tiny, inappropriately named brig called *Speedy* with 14 small guns and 84 men, he had captured the Spanish warship *El Gamo* of 32 heavy guns and a crew of 300. In command of the frigate *Pallas* between 1804 and 1806, he was so successful in raiding enemy commerce that his ship was nicknamed the 'Golden' *Pallas*, and his recruiting posters, which can be seen in the National Maritime Museum to this day, jauntily stated that no man should apply unless he could 'run three miles with a hundredweight of pewter on his back'! In command of the *Impérieuse* in 1808, his activity kept the coasts of Spain and Catalonia in such a turmoil that he became known as the 'Terror of the Mediterranean'. The following year he organized an attack by fireships against a French fleet sheltering in the Aix Roads, and it was only the excessive caution shown by the commander-in-chief, Lord Gambier, that enabled the majority of the ships to escape.

But the single-minded energy that made him an asset in wartime made him a quarrelsome nuisance in peace. Instinctively suspicious of almost everyone in authority over him, his well-publicized criticisms of his superiors were notorious. On becoming a Member of Parliament, he became a leading radical and spent much energy castigating the government and the naval establishment. Universally liked by his subordinates and popular with the underdog, he was seen as a garrulous troublemaker by his superiors. Lord St Vincent, one of the greatest sailors of his age and no less a scourge of naval corruption, complained that Cochrane and his family were 'romantic, money getting and not truth telling'.

Cochrane's interest in money and pecuniary reward was notorious. His father had lost the family fortune in failed scientific experiments, and his son had inherited both his technical interests and his impoverished bank account. It was perhaps understandable that the son of a peer with rank and social position, but without the financial means to sustain them, should be interested in cash. But Cochrane's obsessions with prize money and his assumption that the Admiralty was failing in its duty if it did not send him on lucrative commerce-raiding expeditions were hardly admirable.

In 1814 Cochrane was involved in a Stock Exchange swindle, clearly engineered by some of his more shady relations. A fake colonel arrived in Dover, announced that Napoleon was dead, and took a post chaise up to London, noisily announcing the news on the way. As a result the stock market soared and the conspirators cashed in their shares to make a handsome profit. Unfortunately the 'colonel' went to Cochrane's house in Green Street to change out of his regimentals. Largely on the basis of this evidence, Cochrane alone (his co-defendants having smartly fled the country) was tried for fraud, found guilty and briefly imprisoned. Although he protested his innocence and claimed that the prosecution had been politically motivated, he was disgraced, stripped of his Knighthood of the Bath and dismissed from the Royal Navy. When he emerged from gaol he was therefore only too glad to accept an invitation to leave Britain and command the new Chilean Navy in its struggle for independence from Spain.

The Spanish Navy at this time had command of the Pacific coast, but its mastery was as much the result of patriot inactivity as the size of the forces at its disposal. The Napoleonic Wars had devastated the once proud Spanish Navy. Although winged at Trafalgar, it had really been destroyed by the French occupation, which had effectively crippled its dockyard, shipbuilding and logistical foundations. In 1817 the Supreme Admiralty Council estimated that to defend its worldwide interests, Spain needed a navy of 156 vessels, including 20 of the line, 30 frigates and 44

corvettes and brigs.[3] Only a fraction of this number was available.
Efforts were made to find more. Five small ships were ordered
from France, and behind the backs of his ministers, Ferdinand VII
bought seven warships from his friend the Tsar of Russia. Alas,
with one exception, all were found on arrival to be totally and
embarrassingly rotten. The one sound vessel, a frigate renamed
Maria Isabel, was immediately sent round the Horn convoying
troops, only to be captured by the new Chilean Navy under its first
commander Blanco Encalada. Under her third name, *O'Higgins*,
she was to serve as Lord Cochrane's flagship.

By straining every sinew the Spaniards managed to find warships for Latin American waters but, because of a tactical mis-
judgement, they were sent to the wrong place. Most were deployed
in the Caribbean in support of Murillo. The Pacific coast was
neglected. Indeed, Commodore William Bowles of the British
South America Squadron reported at the end of 1817 that 'the
whole naval force of His Catholic Majesty in these seas consists of
the *Venganza* and *Esmeralda* of 36 guns each, and three corvettes of
16 or 18 guns'.[4] Reinforcements arrived in the shape of the frigate
Prueba, but Spain's other vessels were small and of little military
use. It only took a resolute enemy to mount a serious challenge –
and Lord Cochrane was a resolute enemy.

Arriving in Valparaiso in November 1818, Cochrane was received like a hero. He went immediately on the offensive. In 1819
he concentrated on blockading the coast of Peru, sweeping the
seas of Spanish merchantmen, and making a sally against the naval
base of Callao. In 1820 he turned south, and in February stormed
and captured the last Spanish stronghold on the Chilean coast,
Valdavia. But even at this stage, Cochrane's career in Chile was
beginning to show the same pattern as elsewhere. Brilliant successes were followed by niggling quarrels over lack of pay and the
non-payment of prize money. But in spite of the disputes and
consequent desertions by foreign seamen, the war went on. In
August 1820 the great sea-borne assault on Peru was ready, and
San Martin embarked with his troops on 13 transports and eight
of Cochrane's warships. The following month the army landed
south of Lima to begin its slow encirclement of the Peruvian

capital, while Cochrane enforced a new blockade and threatened the adjacent naval base of Callao. There, in November 1820, he launched a night assault by boats on the Spanish frigate *Esmeralda* and carried her off from the middle of a hostile and heavily fortified harbour. It was one of his most daring and spectacular coups. Indeed, so astonished and angry were the locals that they attacked and murdered a boat's crew from the USS *Macedonian* on the assumption that they must have helped. HMS *Hyperion*, also a witness, kept well out of the way.

San Martin was cautious in his advance against Peru. Time, he knew, was on his side. On 1 January 1820 the Spanish hope of reconquest had been shattered by a mutiny of the troops forming the great Cadiz Expedition. Ferdinand VII's despotic government had been overthrown and the new liberal government had decided on a change of policy in South America. Its commanders were ordered to negotiate a compromise. But with the patriots unwilling to settle for anything short of independence, the only result was to undermine the morale of the Spanish troops in the field. Meanwhile, through 1820 and into 1821, on land and sea, the struggle continued.

CHAPTER 3

THE BRITISH SOUTH
AMERICA SQUADRON

The changes that took place in South America in the wake of the
Napoleonic Wars were not only political. There was a significant
economic aspect as well. The first act of both the Portuguese
monarchy in Rio de Janeiro and of the new revolutionary regimes
in Spanish America was to renounce the old colonial trading
restrictions and to open their ports to the trade of the world –
which, while the wars lasted, meant the trade of Britain. Excluded
by Napoleon from the continent, merchants jumped at the
opportunity. British ships and manufactures poured into the new
markets, filling the harbours, clogging the wharves and
overflowing from the customs houses. With the coming of peace,
Britain's industrial lead ensured that this dominance continued, so
that by 1820 the annual value of exports to South America was
over £3.5 million.[1] Rio de Janeiro, Buenos Aires and Valparaiso
came to resemble emporia of British goods – there were hats,
boots, glassware, linen, cotton, woollens, clothing, firearms,
earthenware, tinplate and manufactures of all kinds. The USA,
specializing in flour and lumber, was in second position, but her
exports were only a quarter of the British figure. Side by side with
trade came local British mercantile communities, establishing
commercial houses, Anglican churches, clubs and cricket. And
with trade and merchants came shipping. In 1820 there were no
fewer than 350 British merchantmen annually traversing South
American waters. It was this trade, these ships and these
communities that found themselves in the front line during the
revolutionary struggles that afflicted the continent after the

Napoleonic Wars.

The instability of the period was of great concern to the British government. The Royal Navy had established a squadron in South American waters as early as 1808, and the independence struggle put enormous burdens on the successive captains and commanders-in-chief. From the beginning, British merchantmen were the victims of both republican privateers and the Spanish authorities, as the latter intermittently embargoed rebel ports. Then with the Spaniards threatening reconquest, and the patriots forming regular navies and imposing blockades, the problem became more grave. The appearance of Lord Cochrane too caused alarm. British naval commanders were well aware of his enthusiasm for both action and financial gain, and feared an unscrupulous onslaught on neutral commerce in the interests of prize money.[2] But, as they later reported, their fears were unfounded – although there were inevitable disputes over the 18 British vessels arrested by Cochrane and the Chilean Navy as blockade runners.[3]

The Americans and the French, the two other nations whose commerce was under threat, also maintained a continuous naval presence in South American waters. The USA felt that a frigate on station at any one time was generally enough to protect its interests, reinforced by a smaller vessel in times of crisis. First there was the *Ontario* (Captain James Biddle), then the *Macedonian* (Captain John Downes), then the *Constellation* (Captain Charles Ridgley) and then, in response to the expedition against Peru in 1820, the 74-gun *Franklin* (Commodore Charles Stewart) supported by the schooner *Dolphin*. France on the other hand, maintained a substantial and changing squadron off South America, its composition ranging from ships-of-the-line to schooners, under the command of one – sometimes two – admirals. At times the size of the force seemed quite out of proportion to the extent of French trade, and neither the local authorities nor British naval commanders could understand its purpose.

But there was more to it than performing normal naval duties. Britain only maintained diplomatic representatives in monarchical Brazil. There were no diplomats in the River Plate, Chile or Peru. Naval officers therefore found themselves acting as floating ambassadors and consuls, reporting to Whitehall on political and military developments, and intervening on behalf of local British communities when either side tried to raise forced loans or attempted to impose unfair commercial regulations. Their dealings were complicated by the need to maintain strict neutrality between Spain, an allied power, and the new revolutionary regimes whose goodwill was needed to safeguard the lucrative British trade in the region, but who knew little of the conventions of war and were sensitive to any supposed slight.

Britain was fortunate to have two outstanding naval commanders-in-chief on the South America station at this time. They were Commodore William Bowles, who served from 1816 to 1819 and had previous experience in the area, and Sir Thomas Hardy, Nelson's Flag Captain at Trafalgar, who began a four-year stint in 1819. Both men were prepared to act firmly when the situation required it, but brought tact, moderation and good judgement to their assignments – enhanced in the case of the former by experience and intelligence, and in the case of the latter by an avuncular good humour.

But not all officers were able to maintain the high-minded neutrality required, and when they fell short the Admiralty was ready to rap them over the knuckles. Captain William Shirreff of the *Andromache*, for example, was rumoured to be so partial to the patriot cause that Spanish protests led to the frigate's return to England.[4] On the other hand, Captain Thomas Searle of the *Hyperion* developed such a distaste for both Lord Cochrane and his activities that the Admiralty was forced to recall him in March 1821. One result was that during the cutting out of the *Esmeralda*, the crew of the *Hyperion* had to watch with cold indifference while the USS *Macedonian* was ringing with cheers and encouragement.

Local British merchants, however, showed their appreciation of the two captains by ensuring that both returned to Portsmouth loaded with money and specie. Shirreff had earned additional gratitude by being a founding father of the Valparaiso Cricket Club. Thomas Collings, clerk of the *Owen Glendower*, reported that Searle was carrying £600,000, while the notoriously high-living Shirreff had £300,000.[5] Since the captains whose ships carried

such 'freight' in peacetime were paid an average of one per cent of
the value (the actual proportion depending on distance) – the same
amount being divided between the commodore commanding and
Greenwich Hospital – they arrived in England richer to the tune of
£6000 and £3000 respectively! Alas, unlike prize money, no-one
else on the ship benefited financially from carrying freight. The use
of warships to safeguard and transport the profits of British trade
in the form of coin and bullion was quite normal. Indeed, they
were constantly available to perform these functions and there was
an understanding that a vessel would be available every four
months or so to carry such remittances round the Horn.[6] In the
South American summer of 1821–22, for example, *Owen Glendower*
returned with £400,000,[7] *Conway* with £220,000,[8] and *Superb* and
Creole with £300,000 each.[9] Hardy himself wrote to friends that he
hoped to return with at least £20,000 as his share of freight money
at the end of his tour of duty.[10] Since Hardy received about ½ per
cent of the total, this would have meant that the South America
Squadron was carrying freight to the value of £4 million during his
initial three-year period of command. Ships of the United States
Navy performed exactly the same functions in respect to American
trade. The *Ontario*, for example, left Chile carrying $210,000
(£42,000) in 1818; the *Constellation* had $320,000 (£80,000) on
board when she sailed from Valparaiso to New York in 1822;
while Captain John Downes – whose obsessive interest in 'freight'
provoked much criticism from American Consul General Judge
Prevost – admitted that when *Macedonian* returned round the Horn
at the end of its tour of duty it had at least $1 million (£200,000) in
coin and bullion on board.[11]

The focus of British government and Royal Navy attention
inevitably changed as the various campaigns unfolded. At first, the
Portuguese invasion of the Banda Oriental and the instability in
Buenos Aires made the River Plate the priority. Then, with the
growing intensity of the independence movements in Chile and
Peru, attention moved to the West Coast. But just as the war in the
Pacific seemed to be reaching a conclusion, a hint of trouble
appeared on the other side of the continent in the great Portuguese dominion of Brazil. With the King firmly in residence and

the country receiving all the administrative and commercial benefits, there had been no independence movement there in the post-war years. But the prosperity of Brazil meant the decline of Portugal, and in August 1820 a military revolt in Oporto put the spark to Portuguese resentment. It led to open rebellion. A liberal constitution was proclaimed, and a democratic Côrtes elected to exercise supreme power. By the end of the year, the British government had become concerned by signs that the constitutional turmoil was spreading to Brazil.

As the political and military situation in Spanish America deteriorated in the years after 1817, the Admiralty regularly reinforced its squadron in the region. Fearful of USA intervention in 1818, Bowles's command had been increased to five – two frigates, two 24-gun ships and a small sloop. Under Hardy the number rose to nine, and in 1820 the squadron comprised the 74-gun ships *Superb* (Captain Adam MacKenzie) and *Vengeur* (Captain Thomas Maitland); the frigates *Creole* (Captain Thomas White), *Hyperion* (Captain Thomas Searle) and *Owen Glendower* (Captain the Hon. Robert Spencer); the sixth rates *Conway* (Captain Basil Hall), *Blossom* (Captain Fred Vernon) and *Slaney* (Captain Donat O'Brien); and the 10-gun *Alacrity* (Commander Henry Stanhope). The 74-gun ships were too clumsy and their draughts too deep to be of much use off the coasts of South America and they were ordered home, but in July a French force under Rear Admiral Jurien, consisting of the ship-of-the-line *Colosse*, the frigate *Galathée* and the corvette *L'Echo* suddenly appeared in the South Atlantic. Its arrival caused apprehension in Chile,[12] although neither Hardy nor anyone else could fathom its purpose.[13] Eventually it sailed away again having demonstrated little but the French inclination to fish in troubled waters. Nevertheless, to be on the safe side, the Admiralty decided that the *Superb* should remain longer.

Orders had, however, been sent for the return of the *Hyperion*, and the *Andromache* was already on her way home. Replacements had to be found. The Admiralty chose first the frigate *Aurora*, commanded by Captain Henry Prescott, then looked around for a second. Still floating in ordinary in the Medway, was *Doris*, teakbuilt, ideal for tropical waters and an obvious choice. Orders were immediately sent to Sheerness to re-copper the frigate and prepare her for sea. Their lordships then turned their attention to selecting a reliable commander. The choice fell on Captain Thomas Graham. Four suitably qualified lieutenants and six Admiralty midshipmen were then appointed. With 90 per cent of officers without employment, there was no shortage of candidates.

CHAPTER 4

HMS *DORIS*: THE SHIP
AND THE MEN

Frigates were probably the most glamorous units in the sailing navy. One of their most important roles was to act as the eyes and ears of the fleet and, in many of the great battles of the era, it was the frigates, scouting ahead to right and left in search of the enemy, that brought the lines of heavy warships into action. That done, they could remain as spectators without dishonour, repeating signals or assisting damaged friends. No-one expected them to take on ships-of-the-line unless the latter were disabled. But the majority of frigates were not tied to a fleet's apron strings. Most were used on detached service, either on their own or in small squadrons, engaged in trade protection or, more likely, in destroying that of the enemy. As sea hunters they were formidable. Low and sleek, they were fast enough to avoid any larger warship, and strong enough to overwhelm anything smaller. A fight with anything of equal size was, however, expected, and the history of the Napoleonic Wars is replete with single-ship actions like *Sybille* and *Forte*, *San Fiorenzo* and *Piédmontaise* or *Shannon* and *Chesapeake*. Success brought instant fame to frigate commanders and promotion to their subordinates, and public confidence in victory grew so great that a series of defeats at the hands of the better-manned and larger American frigates in 1812 caused a national trauma.

But there were more rewards for frigate crews than fame and promotion. The value of captured enemy ships was paid to the taker, either in the form of head money for warships or prize money for merchantmen, and seizing enemy vessels was a frigate's job. To the envy of their less fortunate comrades on two- and three-deckers, frigate captains and their crews grew rich on the proceeds. The *Pallas* under Lord Cochrane gained £200,000 in one cruise. The *Brilliant* commanded by Henry Blackwood received £23,575 for taking the *Eenrom*. And *Triton*, *Alcmene*, *Naiad* and *Ethalion* pocketed £651,694 between them for capturing the Spanish treasure ships *Santa Brigida* and *El Thetis*.[1] Not everyone, of course, was quite so lucky.

Unlike the larger ships-of-the-line with their heavy armaments, double rows of gun ports and tubby profiles, frigates were long and low, and carried their principal battery on a single gun deck with an armed forecastle and quarterdeck above, giving a total of up to 60 guns depending on size. By the end of the Napoleonic Wars, the main armament of frigates ranged from 12-pounder guns on the smaller almost obsolete 750-ton vessels, to 24-pounder cannon carried by the new 1500-ton giants at the other end of the scale. At this stage of the conflict, there were 121 frigates of all sizes in commission out of a total naval strength of 644 ships.

Like all frigates, the 42-gun *Doris* was a post captain's command and had an established complement of 245 – five commissioned officers, eight midshipmen and master's mates, the seven usual civil warrant officers – master, boatswain, carpenter, gunner, purser, surgeon and chaplain, four 'inferior' warrant officers – assistant surgeon, schoolmaster, second master and clerk, 173 petty officers, tradesmen and seamen, 17 volunteers and boys and 31 marines including their officer. Five of the seamen were, however, fictitious. Known as 'widows' men', they were carried in the ship's muster book so that their pay could be retained and used to fund Greenwich Hospital for retired and invalided seamen.

A warship was often at sea for long periods and was a self-contained floating community with a ship's company that included all the skilled men and specialists that she and the crew needed for their many roles. In addition to listing the actual ship's company, the *Doris*'s pay book gives the authorized 'establishment' for a frigate of this type, specifying the disposition of the 240 officers and men as follows:

to sail and administer the ship
    1 captain
    4 lieutenants
    8 midshipmen/master's mates
    1 clerk
    1 master and 1 second master
    1 boatswain, 3 mates and 1 yeoman
    1 captain's coxswain and 1 coxswain for the launch
    6 captains of the mast, foretop, and maintop
    4 captains of the afterguard and forecastle
    5 quartermasters
    1 master-at-arms and 1 ship's corporal
    1 yeoman of signals
    108 seamen
    4 first-class volunteers and 13 boys

to maintain the ship's artillery, powder and small arms
    1 gunner, 2 mates and 8 crew
    31 marines

to deal with the maintenance of the ship's fabric
    1 carpenter, 2 mates and 7 crew
    1 cooper
    1 sailmaker, 1 mate and 1 crew
    1 caulker
    1 armourer and 1 mate
    1 ropemaker

to deal with the spiritual and physical welfare of the crew
    1 purser
    1 captain of the hold
    1 surgeon and 1 assistant
    1 chaplain
    1 schoolmaster
    1 ship's cook, 2 subordinate cooks, 4 stewards
    1 barber
    Total = 240[2]

Organization

Running a ship-of-war was a highly complex operation that required the efficient organization of its manpower. The crew had to be recruited afresh for every voyage, and inevitably possessed a wide range of intelligence, personality quirks, skills and experience. Admiralty regulations laid down that when a new ship was commissioned, the first task of the first lieutenant was to assess the abilities and experience of every recruit and to 'rate' him accordingly as petty officer, tradesman, able seaman, ordinary seaman or landman. These details were then carefully entered in the muster book together with his place of birth, his age, the date he joined the ship and when he left it. Those who were transferred or invalided out were marked 'D' for 'discharged'. Those who died were marked 'DD' – 'discharged dead' – and the numerous deserters were marked 'R' for 'run'. There were also columns to register the issue of slop clothing from the purser's store, and any advance of pay.

The men were then divided into four sections named after the part of the ship in which they usually worked. The station bills of *Doris* have not survived, but Captain Marryat, in a leaflet on manning published in 1822, shows exactly how this was done.[3] The 70 youngest and nimblest men were employed aloft in the sails and rigging of the three masts and were called 'topmen'. Their older and more experienced colleagues were allocated either to a group of 20 'forecastle men', responsible for anchor work and the rigging of the bowsprit, or to a 28-man 'afterguard', who handled the falls of the braces, sheets and running rigging on the quarter-deck. The remaining 16, inevitably the least skilled and intelligent of the men, were designated 'waisters' and carried out the routine drudgery of the ship from their position in the waist.

With mustering complete, the ship's company was divided into two watches, port and starboard, one of which would be on duty both day and night for four-hour stretches while the ship was at sea. These details were entered in the watch bill. Only the ship's tradesmen – coopers, sailmakers, stewards, cooks etc – remained 'unwatched', and these were known unflatteringly as 'idlers'. The station bills were then drawn up, allocating every officer and man to a specified station when the ship was performing a particular manoeuvre. The whole crew, for example, was needed to unmoor and weigh the anchor, and the men had to be carefully distributed – 96 to man the bars of the capstan that raised the anchor, 12 to hook it to the cat head when it emerged from the water and lash it to the side, 40 to manoeuvre the cables as they came into the ship and coil them in the orlop tiers, 40 to handle the messenger cable (which went round the capstan in a continuous loop), another 20 'nippers' to lash it to the anchor cable, and 18 men ready to release the sails and steer the ship to get it moving. Tacking and wearing the ship needed fewer men, while making or shortening sail could often be handled by the watch on duty depending on the number of sails involved.

That done, the quarter bills were drawn up. These allocated each man to a station when the ship was in action. Up to 50 men were selected for small arms and cutlass training to form boarding parties or fire down on an enemy ship from the tops, while the rest were allocated to the crews serving the guns – or to be more precise, pairs of guns, since they were twinned port and starboard. An 18-pounder main deck gun needed 12 men, a 32-pounder carronade, five men. Each crew member was given a specific function – gun captain, rammer, handspike man, loader etc, and doubled as firemen, pumpers, boarders and sail trimmers when necessary.

The *Doris*'s ship's company was also divided into divisions, each under the command of a lieutenant assisted by three midshipmen. The purpose of this was to enable the officers and men to know each other and for the officer to keep an eye on their welfare, health and cleanliness. There were also special musters of clothing to ensure that they were clean and had all the gear appropriate for the climate. The divisional officers kept lists of their men and of their duties, were expected to prevent swearing and drunkenness, and had to ensure that hammocks and clothing were scrubbed and washed on the days appointed. On the *Doris* this was done weekly on Fridays, with additional washdays in the tropics on Mondays or Tuesdays depending on the weather.[4] It was by divisions that the crew was normally mustered every

Sunday for an inspection followed by divine service and, occasionally, by an equally solemn reading of the Articles of War. Then
there was the mess. This was a less formal unit, but probably one
of the most important elements in the social organization of the
ship. Basically it was a small group for eating and relaxation,
consisting of a group of friends gathered round a table slung
between the guns or in some other cubby hole on the lower deck.
Each man took it in turn to act as 'cook' – collecting rations from
the steward, ensuring that they were cooked in the ship's galley,
and then delivering them to this messmates. Messes were self-
selecting and wise captains were content to allow the men to pick
their own mess mates to complement the official organization of
the ship with a more social aspect.

The isolation of naval life gave seamen idiosyncrasies of dress,
speech and behaviour that marked them out from those on land,
and led to the image of the good-hearted simpleton. In fact, this
reputation was undeserved. Seamen were highly skilled artisans,
thriving in a very tough environment, and required to master all
the complications of rope work, handling sails and steering their
vessel. Whatever his rank, life was hard for everyone on board a
wooden warship, which could be absent for long periods and
subject to all the hazards of the sea and of intermittent action.

But the harshness of life on a man-of-war in comparison with
the lot of working men in other occupations should not be
exaggerated. Life was no less easy for those who were working in
the slums of the new factory towns or in the impoverished
countryside of Regency Britain. And in relation to equivalent
professions, it could be argued that service on a heavily manned
warship was considerably less arduous than in the cost-conscious
merchant service. Manned in order to fight as well as to sail, *Doris*
had a crew of 245. An East Indiaman of equivalent size and sailing
capabilities had no more than 75. Thus, although there were
periods of intense effort on a man-of-war, in peacetime there was
little of the consistent overwork notorious on merchant ships.
Perhaps it was for this reason that the merchant service had to pay
able seamen £3 10s (£3.50) a month – double that offered in the
Royal Navy. Likewise, although naval pay was by no means

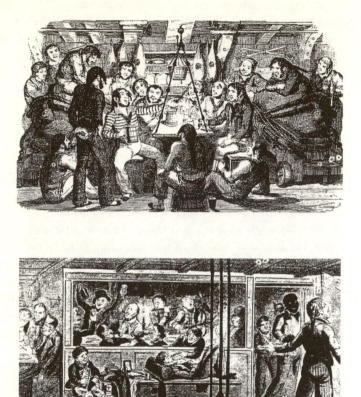

5 A seaman's mess (above) and the midshipmen' berth (below)
Engravings from the National Maritime Museum

generous, it was competitive with rates on land. When *Doris* began
to recruit, the monthly pay of an able seaman was £1 14s (£1.70),
and of civilian warrant officers around £4. On land the average
agricultural wage was estimated to be £1 17s (£1.85), and the pay
of skilled workers like masons, shipwrights and bricklayers was
£6.[5] But from this they had to pay for food and rent.

Food and drink

There were, moreover, various aspects in which life at sea
compared favourably with the lot of those who were employed on
land. In a warship the food was ample even if it was monotonous
and there were problems of preservation – hence stories of sailors
having to knock the weevils out of biscuits, or claims that salt beef
was more suitable for carving models than eating. But the problem
only arose at sea, and ships normally spent between a half and a
third of their working lives in port where fresh provisions were
supplied. *Doris*, for example, was at sea for only 427 days out of
1250 days between July 1821 and December 1824. And the level of
rations was adequate – if not generous – for a working man of the
time. What farm or town labourer could expect a regular weekly
ration of seven pounds of bread or biscuit, four pounds of beef
and two of pork, two pounds of dried peas, 12 ounces of cheese
and one and a half pounds of oatmeal, garnished with butter,
sugar, vinegar and fresh vegetables? Not to mention half a pint of
rum or 1 gallon of beer a day. William Cobbett making his *Rural
Rides* at exactly this time, found that the average agricultural
labourer was lucky to get meat once a week. James Kay,
investigating the condition of factory hands in Manchester, found
the same.[6] And the quantities of meat, cheese, beer and tobacco
given to sailors were three times greater than the average
Northumberland miner could afford, or indeed than were needed
by a working man earning 21s a week according to Mrs Rundell's
best-selling cookery book of 1824, *A System of Practical Domestic
Economy*.[7] Only in regard to bread, butter and sugar did working
men on land do better than those at sea.

Recruitment and desertion

If ease of recruitment is anything to go by, then the seafaring population was fully aware of these advantages. The muster rolls of *Doris* and of the other ships on the South America station show that these vessels were always fully manned, and indicate that the Navy at this period had few problems in recruiting men either at home or overseas. The only exception was HMS *Cambridge*, which arrived early in 1824. However, this was untypical and – as Surgeon John Cunningham describes in his journal – was due to confusion in her fitting-out and last-minute changes in sailing orders. The other ships of the squadron found recruitment easy, but at the same time, desertion continued to be a problem.

The general picture within the Navy as a whole is exemplified in John Byrn's examination of the Leeward Islands Squadron in peace and war between 1784 and 1812.[8] Taking a sample of 73 ships out of a total of the 417 on the station, he calculates that seven per cent of the crews deserted over an average two-year tour of duty. During *Doris*'s 1821–24 commission, 52 men successfully 'ran' out of a total ship's company of 401 – a figure of 14 per cent over four years. More surprising is the number of men who deserted even before the ship left England. On *Doris*, 30 men – or 13 per cent of the 223 on the roll at that time – deserted within weeks of being recruited. Of these, 24 disappeared as soon as they received an issue of clothing and before the ship had been able to make deductions from their salaries to pay for it! This seems to support the claim made by Captain Basil Hall in his memoirs that there was a group of professional swindlers who signed up to do just this, but the circumstances of the men who jumped ship in South America suggest that desertion had more to do with the fecklessness of the seagoing population than with any intent to defraud, or the Navy's working conditions or its disciplinary system. Indeed there is no correlation between desertion and punishments. Interestingly enough, the proportion of deserters who absconded in the first six months of the ship's tour of duty (52 per cent) is the same as that found by Byrn in the Leewards Islands and by Nicholas Rodger in his study of desertion during the Seven Years' War.[9]

Crime and punishment

In the mind of the general public, however, the Navy continued to be unpopular and had a reputation for harsh conditions and brutality. In wartime it had been the press gang, forced recruitment and the uncertainty as to when a man would put his feet on land or see his family again that provoked horror. In peacetime it seems to have been the system of punishments. In the Royal Navy, discipline and punishments were regulated by the Articles of War, supplemented by *Regulations and Instructions Relating to His Majesty's Service at Sea*. The first was a document specially enacted by Parliament to establish a legal framework for conduct and discipline on board ships, and comprised 36 articles divided into four broad categories. One covered crimes against the king and the government (consorting with an enemy, spying, mutiny, embezzlement of public property etc). Another was concerned with offences against individuals (such as murder, theft and fighting). A third covered offences against morality and religion (blasphemy, buggery etc). A fourth – clearly aimed more at the officers than the men – dealt with particular naval infractions (cowardice, failing to do one's utmost, disobedience to orders etc). Hanging, flogging, dismissal from the service and disrating were the most common of the sanctions that were laid down, their application depending on the seriousness of the offence.

As authorities such as Byrn and Rodger have argued, in spite of their special maritime ingredients, the Articles of War were essentially an extension of the civilian criminal code that operated on land to the circumstances of life at sea. Both reflected the prevailing penal theory, which was based on the need to defend society as a whole by threatening the minority of malefactors with painful punishment. Discipline at sea was inevitably different to that which prevailed on land, but it was neither more harsh nor more brutal. Indeed, it could be argued that it was less so. As Nicholas Rodger points out in *The Wooden World*, there were at least 200 offences in the criminal code on land for which capital punishment was prescribed – many for minor crimes against property. In the Navy, there were fewer then 20 capital offences, all of them for serious offences like mutiny or murder, and in only eight cases was hanging mandatory.[10]

Just as the code of law at sea reflected that on land, so did its administration. A system of formal courts martial paralleled the quarter sessions and assizes, and at a lower, summary level, captains acted in a similar capacity to magistrates. Both administered a draconian criminal code with flexibility and even moderation. In 1820, for example, only 107 of the 1129 death sentences handed down by the civil courts were actually carried out; and in the Leeward Islands, only 12 of 26 condemned men were actually hanged.

The differences between naval and civilian justice, however, show up clearly in the statistics. During 1820 the criminal courts of England and Wales handed down 9318 sentences – 1700 of which were for transportation, 5500 for imprisonment (a combined total of 77 per cent), and 1129 (12 per cent) for hanging.[11] By comparison, the figures for the Leeward Islands Squadron, which deployed a third of a million men between 1784 and 1812, show 328 court martial sentences of which 156 were for flogging (47 per cent), 146 for dismissal or demotion (44 per cent), and 26 for death (8 per cent). The difference between the two systems seems to lie not in the idea that one was more harsh than the other, but in the predominance of lengthy incarceration on land as opposed to short, sharp corporal punishment at sea.

Flogging

Flogging is the aspect of naval punishment that provokes the most horror. The Admiralty and its commanders were clearly sensitive to this and were quick to intervene if the level of punishments went beyond that which was regarded as acceptable. Nevertheless it was undoubtedly gruesome, particularly flogging round the fleet (the administration of 300 lashes by instalments before each ship comprising the squadron), which courts martial frequently handed down as a more 'lenient' alternative to the death sentence. It has to be said, however, that, justly awarded, the practice of flogging was widely accepted by seamen at the time and continued in force even during the Spithead and Nore Mutinies when the men themselves were in charge. What seemed to provoke criticism was not so much the principle of flogging, but the fact that in the Navy – unlike the army – it could be awarded arbitrarily without court martial. In a parliamentary debate on flogging in 1825, it was the fact that the punishment could be awarded by the 'arbitrary caprice of commanding officers' rather than by the process of law that was denounced most severely by the radical Joseph Hume.[12] Hume was right. Flogging was by far the most common form of punishment carried out on board ship without the benefit of trial. In his sample of 73 vessels on the Leeward Islands station, John Byrn calculates that there were 6776 such floggings, involving 9 per cent of the men, of which 60 per cent were of a dozen lashes or fewer, and only 12 per cent of three dozen or more.[13] It is interesting to note that the punishment record of Captain Hugh Pigot (notorious for the arbitrary cruelty that provoked a bloody mutiny on the *Hermione*) shows a very similar pattern when he was in command of the *Success* in 1795.[14]

Nevertheless in the post-war period the Admiralty, while believing that corporal punishment was vital to the maintenance of both the Navy's discipline and morale, showed itself increasingly sensitive to the public notoriety of corporal punishment. In recognition of this concern, the practice of running the gauntlet was done away with in 1806; 'starting' – that is seamen being beaten by petty officers with a rope's end – banned in 1809; and 'flogging round the fleet' abolished in 1824. And the records of the South America Squadron in the 1820s show that both the Admiralty and its commanders-in-chief were vigorously trying to regulate the amount of flogging that took place on board ships. Captains had been required to make regular returns of punishments since 1811, and the authorities were quick to take action if they revealed an excessive use of the lash.

HMS *Doris* was a case in point. In the first year of her commission in South America, there were 29 floggings involving ten per cent of the crew – almost the same percentage, incidentally, as in the Leeward Islands. But the astonishing thing is the severity of punishments in Captain Graham's time. It was, after all, peacetime and all the men were volunteers. On *Doris* the 'average' flogging was of 45 lashes: 60 per cent of punishments involved 36 lashes or more; and only 16 per cent were of 12 or fewer – exactly the reverse of the record of the Leeward Islands Squadron.[15] There is nothing in the reputation or character of the officers on the *Doris* to account for this severity of punishment, and it is notable that the number of floggings dropped quickly when the voyage to South America began and the ship's routine became more established. But the average unfortunately shot up again when the frigate reached Bahia and six men attempted to desert. On 14 November they were given eight dozen lashes each.[16]

Nevertheless *Doris*'s record was so extreme that it attracted attention. When Sir Thomas Hardy saw the figures in the quarterly returns, he sent an immediate reprimand for the severity of the punishments.[17] And when the figures arrived in London the Admiralty in its turn demanded an explanation from Captain Graham.[18] Unfortunately by the time the request arrived, Graham was already dead. But the rebuke from on high, and the arrival of a succession of captains with different ideas, caused a change in the situation. It also became established that desertion was no longer a flogging offence. Absconding from the ship was now regarded as 'straggling' – the lesser offence of being absent without leave – and was dealt with by an automatic deduction of £3 from the culprit's pay. The amount of the penalty was always the same and was not changed to take account either of the absconder's rank or the number of times he had 'run'. Thus during the last two and a half years of *Doris*'s commission, the number of floggings fell to 71 involving 1746 lashes (that is, an 'average' of around two floggings a month, and 24 lashes per flogging). The lack of further comment implied that this level was acceptable.

Joseph Hume was right on another point – that the level of punishment depended to a large extent on the attitude, even whim, of senior officers. The punishment records of *Doris*'s four different commanding officers in South America show the contrast clearly. Likewise, if Captain Graham of *Doris* was inclined towards severity, then Captain Thomas Brown of *Tartar* took the opposite line. According to the hard-bitten 'Passed Midshipman' Henry James, good men were being tempted to enlist in Lord Cochrane's

Brazilian Navy because a fair proportion of the *Tartar*'s crew were insolent, drunk or too lazy to do their duty – and were allowed to get away with it. 'The best men in consequence have all the work', he wrote in his journal, 'and I have heard many say that they wished to be with a severe captain for a few months to bring the lazy rascals in!' 'All of this', he concluded gloomily, 'is owing to not using the cat, and if that is not used soon and severely I expect some night they will be taking the ship from us.'[19]

Health

The health record of the South America Squadron in the post-war period shows a remarkable improvement over what was experienced during most of the eighteenth century. First and foremost, the causes of scurvy – the debilitating and eventually fatal scourge of earlier ocean voyages – had been identified and remedied by the supply of Vitamin C. Papers from the South America Squadron do not even mention scurvy, and *Doris*'s log shows that lemon and lime juice, supplemented by vegetables – and fruit in the tropics – were now routine elements in the seaman's diet. South America was also a comparatively healthy station. It was free from the epidemics of yellow fever that decimated warships in the Caribbean and West Africa, although men were still subjected to occasional mosquito-borne diseases in the tropical harbours of Brazil. Rapid movement between widely different climate zones also took its toll.

In addition to dietary changes, much of the improvement can be attributed to the fact that officers now devoted much more attention to the hygiene and cleanliness of the men, their clothing and living accommodation. The men themselves were also more healthy and the ease of recruitment in the post-war period made it easier to reject the sickly and undernourished. But the very nature of life at sea in a crowded wooden ship was hardly conducive to robust good health. The breezes above decks may have been bracing, but below, the ship's company continued to live, eat and sleep in overcrowded, airless and damp conditions. The effects of excessive dampness had, however, been more widely recognized and fewer captains insisted on the continual swabbing of the lower decks with water.

The surgeon's log of the *Doris* has not survived, and it is therefore impossible to know the length of her sick list, the major causes of illness and the success or otherwise of the treatment provided. What we do know is that out of the 480 officers and men who served on the frigate between 1821 and 1825, 63 were invalided out (40 of them after she left Plymouth) and there were only eight fatalities due to natural causes – a remarkably low figure.

Fortunately one surgeon's log from the South America Squadron still exists – that of the sloop *Blossom* of 26 guns, a ship's company of 110 men and a total muster roll of just over 200. In the final two years of her tour of duty from July 1822 to June 1824, her sick list is recorded as 205, of which 198 were restored to duty, six were invalided out and one died. Of this total of 205, four per cent of illnesses were attributed to fever, 19 per cent to accidents, 16 per cent to digestive and bowel complaints – no doubt produced by the remorseless diet of salt meat – and 42 per cent to damp-related complaints such as catarrh, colds and rheumatism. The remaining 19 per cent were attributed to a scatter of different physical causes – notably hepatitis, haemorrhoids, ulcers, strictures and spasms. There is no reference to the 'fluxes' or 'cholera and bellyache' that were such a feature of sick lists during the Napoleonic Wars.

In his report, Acting Surgeon MacDougall described *Blossom* as an exceptionally healthy ship and was in no doubt as to the reason. Notwithstanding what appears at first sight to be a high proportion of illnesses related to damp, he wrote:

> the healthy state of the *Blossom* I am inclined to ascribe to the dry state of the ship, throughout the worst weather the lower deck is perfectly free from moisture. Every attention is of course paid to change the dress of the people as the climate indicated. The lower deck was not washed at stated periods as is the custom in some ships whether the weather is favourable or not, but a dry clear atmosphere was selected and the people prevented from going onto the lower deck during the whole day. I am of the opinion that the constant washing and slopping of the decks is frequently

the cause of large sick lists ... and have formed it on the experience of eleven and a half years of constant employment.[20]

All ships were subtly different in terms of their routines, build and the way they behaved in a seaway, but the nature and composition of *Blossom*'s sick list gives a good indication of the patterns of illness that the ship's company of *Doris* was likely to have experienced on the South America station.

CHAPTER 5

PREPARING FOR SEA: MARCH TO AUGUST 1821

Captain Thomas Graham was a competent and experienced officer who had had a useful but undramatic career in the Napoleonic Wars. A calm and quiet man, he was blessed with what his wife described as a 'gentle modesty' and demeanour. He was already acquainted both with the *Doris* and with Bombay, which had been the scene of some of the most significant events in his life. As a lieutenant he had been sent out in 1808 to join HMS *Russell* in Indian waters and had been a passenger on the same ship as Captain George Dundas, then travelling to begin a four-year term as Navy Board Commissioner in Bombay in company with his 23-year-old daughter Maria. Although Maria was not strong physically and suffered from regular bouts of ill health, intellectually she was robust, opinionated and articulate. Thomas Graham was a fellow Scot, being the second son of the 12th Laird of Fintrey. His eldest brother – with whom there was a happy reunion when the ship stopped at the Cape – was with his regiment in South Africa, serving with such distinction that the city of Grahamstown was named after him. Thomas had got to know Miss Dundas at a literary soiree in Edinburgh, but on the way to India she made a more decisive impact. On the long tropical nights of the voyage, romance blossomed over translations of Tacitus, mutual enjoyment of Scott's *Marmion*, and discussions of Stewart's *Philosophy of the Human Mind*, and when the couple stepped ashore into the heat and dust of Bombay they were engaged. They were married on 9 December 1809.

Thomas Graham was promoted to commander in 1810, taking

charge first of the receiving ship *Arrogant*, then the gun-brig *Hecate*, then the sloop *Eclipse* – all serving with *Doris* in Indian waters under Pellew. In July 1811 his good fortune continued with further promotion to captain in order to take the recaptured frigate *Africaine* back to England. Meanwhile Maria, in between minor attacks of consumption, was completing her *Journal of a Residence in India*. She followed her husband a few months later, using the voyage to polish up the drafts of the book, which was published in 1812. By this time Captain Graham was in American waters with the frigate *Laurestinus*, taking part in the blockade of the Chesapeake, and in attacks on Hampton Roads until the ship was wrecked on an uncharted reef during a storm. He then took temporary command of the prize USS *Chesapeake*, captured after her dramatic duel with HMS *Shannon*.

Peace left Captain Graham without employment. He and Maria lived first at their family home near Edinburgh, then in London. Father George Dundas had returned to Britain in 1812, his steady progression up the Captain's List having continued until he was eventually made Rear Admiral of the Blue in August 1814. Having achieved this professional peak, he promptly died, leaving Maria £5000 and a legacy of £100 a year – a useful supplement to Captain Graham's annual half pay of £220. The couple visited Italy in company with the artist Charles Eastlake (which resulted in *Three Months Passed in the Mountains of Rome during the Year 1819*) and were settled near Plymouth when the offer came to command HMS *Doris* on the South America station. Thomas Graham not only accepted the appointment but, to the gratitude of posterity, decided to take Maria along with him.

Captain Graham arrived in Sheerness to commission the *Doris* on 2 April 1821, taking over from the warrant officers who had maintained the frigate in reserve. They had also supervised her re-coppering at a cost of £13,337.[1] The Purser, Bartholomew Worth, was also on board. Not only had he 25 years' experience, but was an old shipmate of Captain Graham, having served and been wrecked with him on the *Laurestinus* in the American War. Three days later the frigate left dry dock for a mooring in the river. The sheer hulk was brought immediately alongside to begin the hefty task of lifting her heavy lower masts and bowsprit into position. Ninety-nine tons of additional ballast were then loaded and positioned, and the work of fitting her out for sea began in earnest. By the end of the month, her topmasts had been swayed up and fitted, the lower yards were in position and, with decks littered with pitch, hemp, and cordage, the riggers and the crew set up the main and topmast stays and shrouds, covered them with protective Stockholm tar, and crossed them with ratlines. Then they made a start with the topsail yards and the running rigging.

At the beginning of May lighters came alongside to pump 64 tons of water into the frigate's tanks, and boats began to ferry out stores and provisions brought from the victualling yard. Within days, the *Doris* was loaded with beef, pork, bread, flour, tobacco, butter, raisins, sugar, cocoa, peas, oatmeal, lime juice, lemon juice, red wine, brandy and rum. The barrels containing each item were carefully numbered by Purser Worth and stowed in identified places in the hold.[2] He also took delivery of bales of hammocks, bedding, and 'slop' clothing so that the men could be clad in the manner laid down by the Admiralty. This consisted of one canvas or beaver hat, two neckcloths, four pairs of stockings, six shirts, two blue woollen jackets and 'trowsers', waistcoats, Guernsey frocks, flannel drawers, a long all-enveloping pea-jacket and two pairs of shoes. Ships like *Doris* that were heading for the tropics also carried warm-weather alternatives in the form of frocks and trousers made of white duck, and straw hats. In terms of under-garments, however, there were no concessions made for the heat. Prevailing medical opinion continued to stress the need to wear flannel next to the skin whatever the temperature. The cost of the slop clothing and bedding issued to the men was met through deductions from pay, and Worth kept careful records to show what had been distributed and what was remaining in store.[3] Mrs Graham was also on board. She was busy organizing the captain's accommodation, ordering a library of books from her publisher John Murray, dealing with the extra stores they would need, and was, as she wrote to friends, 'head in a whirl over geese, ducks and fowls, and up to the ears in pickles and preserves'.[4]

Of the frigate's total complement of 245 officers and men, 107 were now on board including First Lieutenant J. Wylde with 29 Royal Marines who had appeared splendid in scarlet and pipe-clay on 11 April. All four of *Doris*'s commissioned officers were also on the ship, They were, in order of rank, Lieutenants James Henderson, William Dance, John Smart and Matthew Lys. The drastic run-down that the Royal Navy had experienced since 1815 had left only 15 per cent of the 3730 available lieutenants with employment. These four must therefore have regarded themselves as lucky. But there is no evidence as to why the Admiralty had chosen them. None seemed to have had 'interest' or pull in terms of being related to politicians, the nobility or naval officers, although Captain Graham may have put in a word for Smart who had served under him as a midshipman on *Hecate* and *Laurestinus*. All, however, had seen extensive service in the late wars. Henderson had joined the Navy as far back as 1796 and had spent 17 years on board frigates in the East Indies, being First Lieutenant of the *Sir Francis Drake* during the storming of the Fort of Sumanap during the conquest of Java in 1811. He had then served in the *Cydnus* on the North America station, taking temporary command when his captain died at sea. Returning from an appointment in the *Owen Glendower* in South American waters, he had been promptly posted to *Doris* to be sent back again. Dance and Smart had both seen service in the East and West Indies, and had been active during the American War, the first on Sir Thomas Hardy's *Ramilles*, the second serving under Sir George Cockburn (now, usefully, a leading member of the Board of Admiralty) where he had been wounded in the capture of Hampton in 1813. Lys had also served in South America and India and had been on the *Minden* during the bombardment of Algiers in 1816. The appointments of all four had the appearance of rewards for past service rather than reflecting any political 'interest' or pull. Indeed, only the gentlemanly Dance achieved any further promotion.

The same is true of the selection of midshipmen. In normal circumstances, a 42-gun frigate had a complement of eight midshipmen and master's mates: *Doris* carried 12. Traditionally, such appointments were in the gift of the captain who, by accepting the sons of friends or the politically influential, helped to extend the networks of interest and mutual obligation so important in Georgian times. In the post-war period, the Admiralty had begun to restrict this prerogative by asserting its right to designate what were called 'Admiralty midshipmen' and to appoint them directly to individual ships. The captains could still make their own appointments, but the Admiralty midshipmen not only received priority in appointments, but took their place on a privileged promotion list. Indeed, if their ships were paid off before the coveted promotion had taken place, then port admirals were required to retain them on the books of the flagship until another seagoing opportunity presented itself.[5]

The scheme was introduced in March 1818, and was seen not only as a way of asserting Admiralty authority, but as a gesture designed to help the legions of wartime midshipmen now in their middle or late 20s, who had passed the lieutenant's examination but had found it impossible to secure an appointment. The Admiralty midshipmen system was extended to graduates of the Royal Naval College at Portsmouth to ensure that they secured postings at sea in spite of the hostility of many captains to 'book learning' as opposed to practical experience. The *Doris* had no 'collegians' on board, but it did have five Admiralty midshipmen and one master's mate – M.C. Forster, Charles Blatchley, James Turner, R.J. Cunningham, William Candler and John Gregory (quickly exchanged with William Glennie, a veteran of Algiers who, in addition to being the son of Dr Glennie, Lord Byron's headmaster at his academy at Dulwich, was by a happy coincidence Maria Graham's cousin). Candler was the son of a well-established Norfolk family whose numbers included high members of the Church of England, but the others seem to have been without political influence. All, however, were long-serving officers between 24 and 26 years old. And in accordance with the wishes of the Admiralty, all but one had become lieutenants on the South American station by the end of 1825, although Cunningham's drunkenness prevented his being confirmed in the rank.[6]

The remaining six midshipmen were Captain Graham's nominees, though only appointed with the agreement of the Admiralty.[7] Socially, again, they were an extremely mixed bunch. Two – Lord

William Paget (son of Field Marshal the Marquis of Anglesey who
had lost a leg commanding the cavalry at Waterloo) and the Hon.
Frederick Grey (member of an influential Whig family and son of
Lord Grey, later prime minister and father of the Reform Bill)
were from the top of the social and political ladder. Within five
years, Paget had become a post captain and a Member of Parliament, while Grey ended his career as an admiral and GCB. But of
the others – Robert Parry, James Brisbane, Jonathan Montgomery
and John Langford – only the last was of any note at all, being the
son of a retired army captain who was a leading Taunton justice of
the peace.

Meanwhile the rest of *Doris*'s warrant officers were arriving.
Thomas Biddle reported as sailing master, the Reverend John
Penny as chaplain, Jonathan Louden as surgeon, a replacement for
the gunner in the shape of John Nesbitt, and four first-class
volunteers – that is, aspirants to the quarterdeck. These were
Charles Bosanquet, son of an FRS who was also deputy Lord
Lieutenant of Essex; Oliver Desauges, nephew of a baronet;
William Maude, whose father was an invalided naval commander;
and Thomas Boxald, son of an Arundel merchant who nevertheless (as Captain Graham anxiously assured the Admiralty) had
'been educated a gentleman'.[8] By the end of June 1821 most of the
frigate's sea officers, civilian officers and senior ratings were in
place.

Captain Graham now turned his attention to finding the 90 or
so men he still needed to complete his crew. The supply of sailors
from Sheerness had been slow from the beginning, so to quicken
the process, on 23 April Lieutenant Smart and Midshipman
Blatchley were sent to London to open a recruitment rendezvous.
The volunteers began to arrive in May and June. By the middle of
July Sheerness had produced a total of 54 men and London
another 105. As they boarded the ship, Lieutenant Henderson
rated them as landmen, able or ordinary seamen, tradesmen or
petty officers, entered them in the frigate's muster book, and
began to draw up the watch, station and quarter bills. In contrast
with the Navy's wartime experience, recruitment proved easy, but
the influx of men from the rendezvous was matched by a steady

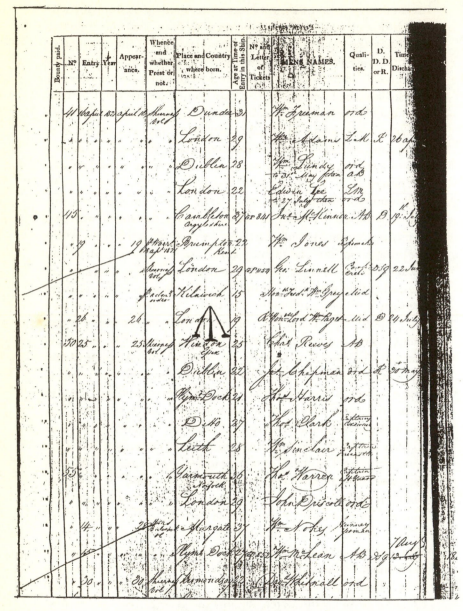

6 Extract from Doris' Muster Book
Public Record Office

stream of deserters. By the time the ship sailed for South America, 30 had disappeared and had to be marked 'R' in the ship's books.[9] Some of these men – volunteers all – lasted less than a fortnight before they decided that a man-of-war was not their cup of tea and disappeared. Not even the issue of clothing and tobacco, and the temptation of six pounds of fresh meat and vegetables, two pounds of peas, and three and a half pints of rum a week could induce them to stay. Of the 212 men raised between March and August in Sheerness and London, only 164 were still on board when *Doris* eventually sailed for South America. Of the rest, 30 had deserted, 13 had been invalided out, three had been transferred and two had died.[10]

The work of preparing the frigate for sea continued with increased intensity. During May, *Doris*'s anchors and cables, both hemp and chain, were ferried to the side and hoisted on board. On the 18th, her sails were brought over from Chatham Dockyard. The sailmakers and their mates toiled for weeks fitting reefing points before they could eventually be hoisted and secured to the yards. Meanwhile, on 21 May, her guns and shot were delivered. Each of her 18-pounders weighed 42 cwt, and each 32-pounder carronade 17 cwt: arming the *Doris* therefore meant the handling of a total of 68 tons of ordnance. Each piece was brought alongside, hoisted by blocks and muscle power to the decks of the frigate, fixed on its carriage or slide and secured with breeching lines and gun tackles to the side. It was heavy work, but there was only one serious accident, on 2 June, when a seaman was killed by a falling block. The incident was made doubly tragic by the fact that his newly married wife was on board at the time.[11]

By the end of May, *Doris* was almost ready. Artisans from the dockyard swarmed over the ship, painting it from stem to stern in its livery of black with a band of white along the line of the gun ports and round the stem. Finally, on 16 June, with her topgallant masts and yards fitted and rigged, the ship left her mooring and moved to an anchorage in the Nore, off Garrison Point. There, with a pause to cheer the passing of HMS *Aurora* also on her way to South America from Chatham, the final tricky task of loading the gunpowder was completed, and the water hoy topped up her tanks to their maximum of 112 tons. Now ready for sea, on 6 July 1821 HMS *Doris* weighed anchor and headed for Portsmouth.

Driven by a brisk north-west wind, which soon turned gusty with sudden squalls of rain, the frigate passed through the throng of shipping in the Downs and turned west past Beachy Head. On 8 July she sighted the low green hills of the Isle of Wight and made her way into the Navy's principal anchorage of Spithead. Taking up a mooring close to the entrance to Portsmouth harbour – Fort Monkton lying north-west by north and Southsea Castle north-east by east – *Doris* took on board her final supplies of bread, pork, butter, sugar, soap and cocoa from the victualling yard, and made last-minute adjustments to the crew. Eleven men had to be medically discharged – six of them to Haslar Naval Hospital – but fortunately, 13 volunteers and two Royal Marines – one a drummer – were found to more than make up for the deficiency. There were also changes among the warrant officers. Both clerks were transferred (one to Haslar) but a replacement arrived in the shape of Henry Broughton, while the ship received a new boatswain called Thomas Bond, and a schoolmaster who was establishing himself as a minor Scots poet by the name of James Hyslop. One midshipman also went ashore. This was Lord William Paget, summoned suddenly to London to wait upon King George IV at the forthcoming coronation.[12]

On 13 July *Doris* was smartened up to receive an inspection by the Commander-in-Chief, Sir James H. Whitshed KCB. Paint was retouched, decks holystoned, brass work burnished, and the rigging set up taught. Although a gang of dockyard artificers was still remodelling the lower deck to accommodate *Doris*'s expanded complement of midshipmen, Whitshed was satisfied with what he found, and was shown to the side by the officers in full dress while the crew manned the yards to give him the appropriate send off. On 19 July there was more excitement when the frigate, in company with other ships in the anchorage, fired a royal salute in honour of King George IV. At the same moment as the thunder of the guns began to roll between the Isle of Wight and Portsdown Hill, George was being crowned King at a coronation of unexampled feudal pomp and splendour. Inspired by his own artistic taste, and backed by a government that realized the value of spectacle in producing loyalty in place of public derision for George's extravagance and his acrimonious feud with his termagant estranged wife Caroline, no expense was spared to produce a vast Gothic spectacle. There was the King's champion in full armour; peers and ministers in white satin, doublets and slashed hose; the Duke of Wellington backing his horse down the steps of Westminster Hall; women scattering herbs before George's gouty feet as he processed under a golden canopy, wearing a crown on his dyed curls and with a huge train of crimson velvet trimmed with gold so heavy that it threatened to pull him off his feet. The ship's company of *Doris* no doubt derived extra satisfaction from the knowledge that one of the nine pages attempting to manoeuvre this massive train was one of their own midshipmen.

Four days later the frigate left her mooring off Portsmouth and moved down to St Helens. As was normal practice for a ship about to sail, a clerk came aboard to hand out a two-month's advance of pay to the crew – £3 4s (£3.20) for able seamen, £2 8s (£2.40) for ordinary seamen and £2 2s (£2.10) for landmen. Unfortunately, adverse winds held up *Doris*'s departure and, with money in their pockets, four more sailors ingeniously took advantage of the boat traffic with the shore to desert! There was one more disappearance, but of a more elevated kind. On 24 July the *Royal George* yacht came out of the harbour preparatory to receiving the new King on board. Her commander, Captain the Hon. Sir Charles Paget, clearly felt that his kinsman would be more suitably employed on the royal yacht than on a work-a-day frigate on the South America station, and had Midshipman Lord William Paget transferred to his vessel. Sir Charles may later have regretted his intervention. Having secured rapid promotion through top-level string-pulling rather than his own efforts, by 1829 Lord William had already fallen into a lifestyle of such profligate extravagance as to reduce his father to despair and force him into semi-permanent exile in France to avoid imprisonment for debt. After 1833 he only appeared in England intermittently to beg from Lord Anglesey, embezzle from his friends, and unsuccessfully sue Lord Cardigan (later to lead the Charge of the Light

Brigade) with alleged adultery with his wife. Regarded as unemployable by the Admiralty, Paget resigned his commission, left England for good in 1846 and died in poverty in 1873. Perhaps three years on *Doris* might have taught him some self discipline. But he lost the opportunity. His place was taken by an officer of more humble origins, Mr Midshipman Fitzmaurice, who was delivered just in time by boat before the frigate fired another royal salute to mark the departure of King George IV for Ireland, and then made sail for Plymouth.

On 4 August, *Doris* sighted the Start and Pawl Point and, guided by a pilot, made her way cautiously through thick mist past the wonders of the new breakwater – still under construction – to an anchorage in Plymouth Sound. The stop was an unscheduled one. In his haste to commission the frigate, Captain Graham had left both personal belongings and unfinished business in Plymouth. A thoughtful Admiralty had given him permission to visit the port on the outward voyage to sort it out.[13] Three days later, having exchanged Midshipman Gregory for Midshipman Glennie, *Doris* was on her way again, thrashing her way past the Eddystone Lighthouse and the Manacle Rocks but forced back by contrary winds to the tiny harbour of Falmouth, the most westerly deep water port on the coast. Final adjustments were made, then on 11 August *Doris*, her colours at half mast to mourn the unexpected death of Queen Caroline, the King's estranged wife, headed for the open sea on the first leg of her voyage to the South Atlantic. On board were Captain and Mrs Graham, a female maid, four lieutenants and a ship's company of 240 men made up as follows:

11 senior/inferior warrant officers
12 midshipmen/mates 52 petty officers/tradesmen
22 volunteers and boys
112 seamen
31 Royal Marines

The crew was complete – indeed she carried five men above the authorized establishment. But there were differences. *Doris* was short of two quartermasters, one boatswain's mate, and three

members of the gunner's crew. On the other hand, she carried
eight midshipmen and boys above complement, the youngest 14
years old. And as a marked contrast to her experience in the
Napoleonic Wars, the frigate was well up to strength in relation to
seamen. Not only that, they were also well qualified and experienced, for of the men on board 47 had been rated as able, 48 as
ordinary, and only 17 as landmen, while their average age was as
high as 26 years. The nationalities of the quarterdeck officers are
not shown in the muster book, but of the 223 members of the
ship's company whose origins are known, 174 were English, 23
Irish, 18 Scots, two Welsh and six 'foreign' – born respectively in
Hamburg, Quebec, Nova Scotia, Jamaica, Demerera and Malta.[14]

Just as the crew was complete, so were the frigate's stores. In
her hold *Doris* carried 107 tons of water, 31,330 lbs of bread and
biscuit, 14,000 lbs of beef, 12,640 lbs of pork, 185 bushels of peas,
30 bushels of oatmeal, 760 lbs of sugar, 1240 lbs of tobacco, 1580
gallons of rum and brandy, 1072 lbs of cocoa, 2100 lbs each of
lime and lemon juice, and quantities of flour, suet, vinegar, butter,
cheese and soap. With her ship's company consuming 1500 lbs of
meat, 1750 lbs of bread, 110 gallons of rum, and 8 tons of water a
week, *Doris* was provisioned for four months at sea. Only supplies
of red wine were deficient, but these, as usual, were expected to be
made up at Madeira.

CHAPTER 6

THE OUTWARD VOYAGE

At 2 pm on 11 August 1821 HMS *Doris* left her anchorage in Falmouth harbour and headed out into the open sea. Just after dusk the speck of light that marked the Lizard was sighted in the darkness to the north-east and the frigate set course for Madeira. Two days later in Portuguese waters past Cape Finisterre, she was lucky to pick up the tail of the north-east trade winds and headed south. Now with a steady breeze on her port quarter, the frigate began to show a fair turn of speed, spreading studding sails and topgallants when the wind weakened, racing through the blue water under reefed topsails when it freshened. On 16 August she logged a good run of 176 miles, an average of seven and a half knots.[1]

On the second day of the voyage the crew was mustered 'by the list'. Mustering was a weekly ritual in which the men formed a double line on the lee side of the upper decks, while the clerk set up a small table on the quarterdeck, the ship's officers behind him. The clerk then called out the names in numerical order as they appeared in the muster book. The first man (number six, since the 'widows men' occupied the first five numbers) was a 19-year-old landman from Deptford called Edward Penny; the last – number 223 when the ship left Falmouth – was a 23-year-old member of the sailmaker's crew from Plymouth, Jonathan Bradford. When his name was called, each man smartly stepped forward, took off his hat and passed to the windward side of the deck while the clerk registered his presence.

Next day came a more disagreeable naval ritual, when the gratings were rigged and the roll of drums called the hands to the main deck to witness punishment. The culprit was Able Seaman John

Hood from Marlborough, who was given 30 lashes at the gangway for drunkenness exacerbated by the shocking crime of 'pissing on the quarterdeck'. This was the first flogging to take place on the voyage, but the fourth since the frigate had left Sheerness. The others had been respectively for desertion, insolence and neglect of duty.[2]

Life in the *Doris* quickly settled down into the normal man-of-war routine as laid down in the Admiralty Regulations. At dawn, the watch on duty soaked the upper decks with sea water, sanded and scraped them with holystones – blocks of sandstone the size of bibles – then swabbed them dry. At 7 am hammocks were piped up, lashed with the regulation seven turns of black twine, and stowed in the netting along the top of the bulwarks (their painted numbers neatly turned inboard). Then, before the change of watch at 8 am, came breakfast, usually lasting half an hour with an extra 15 minutes on Sundays. The forenoon watch that followed was the busiest period in the working day. While the men on duty stood by to trim the sails and attend to the rigging, it was the time when the remainder of the crew were drilled aloft or exercised with the great guns or the small arms and the cutlasses. But first the lower deck was cleaned 'dry' using holystones and sand, and the resulting dust swept away. The problems caused by excessive dampness were now widely recognized, and *Doris*'s lower decks were only washed once a week on Saturdays.

At noon the master, the officers and the midshipmen gathered on the upper decks with their sextants to establish when the sun was at its zenith, then work out their longitude by comparing the ship's noon with that at Greenwich as shown on the chronometer, equating 15 degrees with every hour of difference. Since John Harrison's development of the marine chronometer, navigation seemed to have become child's play and the *Doris* encountered no navigational problems on her voyage. Meanwhile on the lower deck, the cooks of the various messes collected their victuals and the hands ate their dinner, drank their grog and tasted salt beef or pork (from newly opened barrels 269 and 29) for the first time on the voyage. After soaking to remove the salt, the beef was normally eaten with vegetables in the form of a lobscouse stew, while pork was enjoyed with haricot beans or dried peas and suet duff. Dinner concluded, the watch on duty stood by to work the ship, while the watch below dozed and rested in what was the most sacred period of the day.

In the late afternoon of 18 August, a purple smear of land on the horizon announced that *Doris* had made her landfall. As the rocky peaks and wooded hills of Madeira drew near, the frigate took in sail and, as the sun set, dropped anchor in the Roads off Porto Santo. Promptly next morning, boats appeared alongside carrying fresh meat, vegetables and fruit for immediate use, half a dozen live bullocks to provide fresh meat for part at least of the voyage ahead, and ten pipes of the red wine, which was the island's most famous product. The provisions were hoisted aboard by block and tackle, manoeuvred below and stored by the watch on duty. Eight more British sailors also appeared – volunteers from the town and the British shipping in the port. In fact, the frigate was now so replete with men that she was able to discharge two to help out the undermanned merchant brig *Jane* on her voyage home.[3]

Meanwhile the captain's wife took a group of midshipmen ashore to taste the pleasures of the island. With the young gentlemen on mules and Mrs Graham and her maid in a palankeen litter, the cavalcade slowly wound its way out of the town and up a tortuous path past palm trees, cypresses, vineyards and gardens ablaze with blue hydrangea and fuchsia, to where the church of Nossa Senhora de Monte stood out white and brilliant above a green wooded hill. Below them, they could see the roadstead, shimmering in the sunlight, the shipping tiny against the sparkling blue water. Then it was on to the country house of a Mr Wardrope for refreshment and cheerful relaxation. It was night before the party returned, winding its way down the hillside by the light of torches, the muleteers singing to encourage their animals, until the party reached the jetty to board two shore boats for the pull back to the frigate. The following day Mrs Graham was back, touring the principal buildings of the town, admiring the cathedral and the churches, and viewing with solid Anglican disapproval the gruesome relics in the Chapel of the Skulls. As she noted in her

7 View of Madeira. Engraving from *The Naval Chronicle*

**8 A flogging. Engraving by Cruikshank in the National
Maritime Museum**

journal, she was 'not sorry to find that such a monument to bad taste was fast falling into ruin'.[4]

Three days later the *Doris* weighed anchor and set course for the Canary Islands. On 25 August the high peak of Tenerife was sighted jutting dramatically out of the clouds. Completing its approach, the frigate anchored in 40 fathoms by chain cable because of the rocky abrasive bottom, received more fresh meat and vegetables, and got on with the major purpose of the visit – to top up her casks with fresh water. Meanwhile the indefatigable Mrs Graham was on shore again – this time accompanied by Lieutenant William Dance and two midshipmen. On the back of mules, the party made its way up the black lava of the lower slopes to the luxuriant valleys where there were vineyards and farms growing wheat, barley and potatoes. At noon they arrived hot and dusty at the object of their excursion, the famous thousand-year-old Dragon Tree described so enthusiastically in the writings of naturalist Alexander von Humboldt. There they rested, while Maria Graham did a sketch of the venerable tree. Then they descended, this time taking a more scenic route down a verdant valley past the occasional convent and farm, enjoying the hospitality of their Spanish and, occasionally, English owners as they went. Mrs Graham tried to return the favour by offering entertainment on the frigate the following day, but the swell in the anchorage was so great that the majority of the guests were inconveniently sick.[5]

HMS *Doris* was now ready for her crossing to South America. Her water casks had been filled to 110 tons, and at Tenerife she had gained two more recruits – one a seaman volunteer, the other a brown, white-bearded goat with huge udders which was to supply milk for the sick bay and the wardroom coffee. On the evening of 28 August the last of the islands – Gomera, where Columbus had begun his epic voyage in 1492 – slipped astern, and *Doris* headed firmly south-west for the southern ocean.

With the steady breeze of the trades on her quarter, *Doris* made good progress into the tropical zone, with runs averaging 160 miles a day. There were flying fish, sharks and shoals of brightly coloured jelly fish to admire, as well as a swallow and a locust which had somehow crossed the hundreds of miles of sea from the nearest land. For the first week, the crew luxuriated in fresh meat as, one by one, the bullocks loaded at Madeira were slaughtered and eaten. Fishing lines and hooks were then distributed among the men to vary the diet.

Meanwhile, the purser busied himself opening barrels and issuing stores — cask number ten with sugar, number seven with wine, number 291 with beef, number 257 with pork, and number 537 with flour. *Doris* was also a ship-of-war, and to reach a state of preparedness, Captain Graham ordered no fewer than seven gun drills with the main deck cannon and quarterdeck carronades during the four weeks of the voyage.[6] Then, on the fourth day out, there was another flogging — William Goad this time, for 'neglect of duty'. A week later, with the frigate plunging over the blue seas under a full spread of canvas and studding sails to compensate for a slackening in the trade winds, there was another — Robert Loder, 30 lashes for 'skulking and neglect of duty'. The following week there were more. Marine Thomas Murrill received a dozen lashes for 'disobedience and insubordination', while William Goad — in trouble again — was given another 36, this time for 'filthiness and neglect of duty'.[7]

On Sundays there was a change in the daily routine. At 10.30 am the drum beat to divisions and the crew lined the upper decks for an inspection by the captain and the first lieutenant — boys on the forecastle, marines on the quarterdeck, forecastlemen, topmen, afterguard and waisters in between. Sunday — like Thursday — was a 'clean shirt and shaving day', so the men were at their cleanest and most presentable. Inspection complete, the frigate was rigged for divine service — officers in blue and gold on the quarterdeck, red-coated marines lining the bulwarks, the men in their best clothes in the waist. Chaplain Penny recited the rites of the Church of England as laid down by a devout Admiralty, after which Captain Graham read the stirring cadences of the Articles of War. At noon came dinner, followed by a period of leisure for the men until the change of watch at 4 pm, during which they could sit chatting with friends, read, or walk about the ship. Captains traditionally ensured that this sacred time was free from duty as far as the running of the ship allowed.

As the frigate moved further and further south, the days became hotter as the angle of the sun over the deck steadily approached the vertical. Purser Bartholomew Worth issued suitable
outfits of tropical clothing to the crew. On 18 September *Doris*
was approaching the equator and prepared for the traditional
ceremony of 'Crossing the Line'. Triton (played by captain of the
foretop William Sullivan) mounted on a sea-horse 'admirably
represented' and dressed in oakham and swabs, hailed the ship to
be told it was '*Doris*, commanded by Captain T. Graham, on a
man-of-war cruise', and was given permission to come aboard.
Then Neptune (Quartermaster Thomas Clark) with trident and
crown, and Amphitrite (Able Seaman Thomas Ware) mounted in a
sea cart drawn by eight sea horses, appeared accompanied by
painters, constables and barbers all wearing dress appropriate to
their callings plus seaweed skirts imitating fish scales and tails. Mrs
Graham amplified the brief laconic entry in the ship's log:

> After the progress round the decks, a conference with the captain,
> and a libation in the form of a glass of brandy, to which the god
> and goddess vied with each other in devotion, the merriment
> began. Mock-shaving, or a fine paid, was necessary to admit the
> new comers to the good graces of their watery father; and while he
> superintended the whole business, all the rest of the ship's
> company, officers and all, proceeded to duck each other
> unmercifully. None but the women escaped, and that by staying in
> my cabin. [8]

By 11.30 the ship's routine returned to normal. At noon the
officers shot the sun, the hands went to dinner, and Captain and
Mrs Graham entertained the midshipmen in the stern cabin.

For the midshipmen on board, the presence of the captain's
wife was a mixed blessing. It added zest to their trips ashore, and
extra comfort when they were sick, but it meant more work. Not
only did they have to master the basics of their profession –
maths, geometry, and astronomy – from Schoolmaster Hyslop and
Master Biddle, but Mrs Graham was determined to turn them into
educated gentleman as well by amplifying the curriculum and
teaching poetry, literature (both French and English), the history
of Greece, Rome, France and Britain, Bacon's essays, and extracts

from Blackstone's constitutional history.[9] With all this teaching taking place in the fore cabin close under the captain's eye, there was no escape.

Doris had a lucky voyage. In the Doldrums, ships sometimes ran into calms that left them drifting on an oily swell under a harsh blue sky until they were dragged forward by sweating seamen in the ship's boats. *Doris* was spared this problem. All the way across the equator there was a breeze of some sort, often with thunder and lightning at night. Maria Graham spent many evenings on deck enjoying the experience of a frigate under sail in the moonlight, and reflecting that, of the many authors who had made the attempt, only Lord Byron had succeeded in doing justice to the poetic nature of the sailor's existence. She then enjoyed the sound of the songs and entertainments with which the crew passed the evening watch. Humorous songs were popular and well received, but the preference was clearly for sentimental, tear-jerking ballads. Mrs Graham noted that the current favourite seemed to be a mournful patriotic ditty called 'The Death of General Wolfe'.

Soon the frigate reached the belt of trade winds in the southern hemisphere and put on speed heading south-west. On 13 September in the tropics she had logged less that two knots. A week later, tearing forward on the port tack under studding sails, topsails and royals, she registered a day's run of 192 miles – an average of eight knots. But the speed was not without cost. Ordinary Seaman Martin Mullins fell into the sea from the topsail yard and was drowned before the ship could launch the cutter and come to his aid. Then, on 21 September, the coast of Brazil was sighted. Reducing sail and bending her anchors in preparation, *Doris* made her approach, edging closer to the shore past the high rugged promontory of St Augustin with its red cliffs and distinctive white church. Next day she dropped anchor off the port of Recife, capital of the Portuguese province of Pernambuco.

CHAPTER 7

PERNAMBUCO AND BAHIA

Pernambuco was the richest and most important province in north-eastern Brazil. Occupied by the Dutch in the early seventeenth century, it had been reconquered by the Portuguese to become wealthy on the proceeds of a slave economy producing an abundance of cotton, coffee and, most notably, sugar. The demand for its produce and the fertility of its soil soon made the province the centre of a thriving international trade conducted through the city of Recife, a natural harbour protected from the Atlantic swell by a chain of parallel reefs. To the traveller, the sight of Pernambuco's blue seas, palm-fringed beaches, great plantations and whitewashed towns set among the richly wooded countryside seemed tranquil and enchanting. But beneath the surface lay a tradition of political radicalism and fierce regional loyalty, the latest manifestation of which had been a violently suppressed revolt against the Portuguese crown in 1817.

The news that a constitutional revolt had broken out in Portugal arrived in northern Brazil in January 1821 and, by March, had reached Rio de Janeiro. The ministers of King João VI dithered, uncertain as to what to do, but local Portuguese merchants and troops seized the initiative, took to the streets and forced the monarch to accept the new constitution. Back in Portugal, the Côrtes was convinced that their country's malaise was due to the absence of the monarch and in April, on its orders, the timid and apprehensive King boarded a warship to take him back to Lisbon. Behind him as Regent, he left his eldest son, Pedro, in charge of a country that was teetering on the brink of a political abyss. For the Brazilians had smelt a rat. It had become all too clear that part of the constitutionalist agenda was to reassert the power of Portugal, and to remove the political and commercial advantages that Brazil had enjoyed since 1808. In the south, Brazilian politicians began to prepare a campaign of resistance. And Pernambuco, with its radical traditions, was not slow to follow. Its governor, a stern old soldier called Luis do Rego, who had ruled the province since 1817, was sympathetic to the liberal cause. But in the charged political atmosphere of the time it was not enough. In August 1821 a Brazilian uprising broke out in the interior and a patriot junta was established. Soon the whole of Pernambuco was in turmoil.

It was at this moment that *Doris* appeared in the roadstead. At first her officers were puzzled as to why it took so long for a pilot to appear, or for the fort to respond to their 13-gun salute. But the boats and jangada rafts, which surrounded the frigate selling fruit and knick-knacks, soon told them of the position – Recife was under siege. Hurried visits by Deputy Consul Williams and the governor's aide confirmed the news. The protected waters within the reef were still filled with vessels of all nations – including the packet *Swiftsure*, about to sail for England – but the town was silent and empty, the shops shut, and foodstuffs in short supply except for jerked beef and fish. It was two days before the Captain was able to establish official communications and pay his official calls. Mrs Graham was not far behind, landing – against all advice – on 24 September with Lieutenant Dance and Midshipmen Grey and Langford to pay her respects to Madam do Rego in the bustle and confusion of the Governor's headquarters. Although Dance was the only officer on the ship who could speak either French or Portuguese, there was no problem. Madam do Rego's grandmother had been Irish and she spoke English fluently, while the General himself had learned enough when serving with the Duke of Wellington in the Peninsular War to get by.[1]

That done, the party went on a tour of Recife. They wandered through the empty narrow streets with their tall houses, looking at the public buildings, the churches and convents, the forts and the stone bridges that linked the series of islands on which the city was built. Each gateway was guarded by troops with loaded cannon. Finally they stumbled on a small slave market, the first that any of the party had ever seen. With the city under curfew and slaves confined to quarters, there was little to see – just a few dozen young blacks lying in the street with all the evidence of starvation and long confinement in a slave ship – but it was enough to fill Maria Graham and the midshipmen with profound indignation.

At the urgent request of the Consul and the local merchants, Captain Graham agreed to remain in Pernambuco until the political threat to British interests had passed. That done, *Doris* settled down to make the most of the visit. The weeks that followed were agreeable. There were trips to the houses of English merchants in the town, and excursions on horseback into the green and verdant countryside as far as the Brazilian outposts. There was even a diplomatic incident to sort out when patriot forces refused to allow the *Doris*'s laundry – sent inland to be washed in the luxury of fresh water – to return through their lines. Lieutenant Dance led an expedition to sort things out, which Maria Graham typically insisted on joining. For travellers who had been long confined aboard ship, the journey into the interior of Pernambuco proved to be delightful. First, the party crossed the bridge that spanned the waterway protecting the city, passed through the palm and tamarind trees which fringed the marshes on the other side, then rode through the green countryside to Brazilian-held territory. There they were met by a ragged detachment of troops and were escorted for another five or six miles to the patriot headquarters. Riding against a backdrop of low wooded hills, the party wended its way through a spring landscape of exotic gardens, groves of oranges and lemons, green mandioc fields and scattered homesteads hedged with woven palm leaves interspersed with passion flower and clematis. Finally, they breasted a low ridge to find themselves in sight of their destination – a large white courtyarded mansion standing on the banks of a wide river. There they were ushered into the presence of the junta whose members, relishing the presence of an official British delegation, subjected it to a long and formal recital of Brazilian grievances before agreeing that the *Doris*'s laundry was indeed neutral in the conflict and could be released.[2] Then, with sunset approaching and their mission accomplished, the party remounted and retraced its steps to Recife.

On 30 September the Governor and Mrs do Rego gave an official dinner at their residence for Captain Graham, his lieutenants and the foreign consuls in Recife. They were joined later by a group of leading citizens and officers from the recently arrived French warship *Sappho*, and the evening ended with some agreeable music and enthusiastic toasts to the kings of Portugal, Great Britain and France. In return, *Doris* offered dinner to Consul Parkinson and the leading British merchants, while Mrs Graham entertained the Governor's family and other friends on board with refreshments and fireworks. The success of the occasion was only marred by the fact that the frigate was anchored outside the reef and subject to the discomforting force of the Atlantic swell.[3] Her draught was too great for her to shelter within.

Meanwhile life on board *Doris* went on as usual. The crew were busy with routine maintenance to the rigging, yards and paintwork ('engaged about the ship as the Service required', to quote the log), the armourers working at the forge repairing ironwork, sailmakers refurbishing reefing points, and the purser receiving supplies. There was even a flogging – Landman Charles Knowling for drunkenness and mutinous behaviour. And whatever scarcities may have existed on shore, the efficient victualling arrangements of the Royal Navy went on apace. Every day 260 lbs of fresh meat and 140 lbs of vegetables and fruit appeared alongside to be loaded on board. To vary the diet, the ship's boats were sent out to catch fish, though returning without much success.[4] With Recife in a state of siege, no-one was rash enough to desert. Indeed, *Doris* gained four more British seamen when Captain Graham managed to secure their release from the local gaol where they had been locked up without trial for 16 months on suspicion of privateering.[5]

After ten days anchored off Recife, *Doris* left for a brief cruise along the coast. Mr Dance led a party ashore to arrange for new supplies, returning not only with bullocks, but with a brightly coloured green parrot for the captain's wife; while the Sailing Master Thomas Biddle, and Midshipman Glennie were sent off in the launch to conduct a survey and improve the charts of the area.

The expedition was not a success. The officers were arrested by suspicious sentries; then, on their return, they managed to drop the azimuth compass overboard.[6] More successful was a boat trip by the midshipmen to Coconut Island organized by Mrs Graham and Mr Dance. While the seamen unloaded supplies and organized a picnic under the shade of the palms, the younger members of the party turned their attention to exploring the island, collecting plant specimens and admiring the exotic shellfish on the rocks, the humming birds among the gaudy flowers, and the gigantic insects and lizards on the sand. The older midshipmen went off with their guns, returning later with a gratifying bag of brightly coloured finches and red-crested woodpeckers. Just as thrilling was the return trip. Instead of the long pull up the lagoon, round the reef and back down to the anchorage, Mr Dance led the three boats in a headlong dash into the crashing surf, and safely through a gap in the coral to where the frigate lay on the other side.

The fun over, HMS *Doris* returned to Recife on 8 October to find that the two sides in the Brazilian conflict had signed an armistice. The streets were now teeming with people and bustling with activity. The officers went ashore to see the sights, sampling the jerked beef with mandioc stew which was the regional special-ity, and savouring the variety of nut- and fruit-flavoured sweet-meats which were brought in from the interior in little kegs. Mrs Graham was forcibly struck by the large proportion of mulattos and blacks – many of them fat and apparently affluent – in the population.[7] But it was time to go. The reason for the frigate's prolonged stay had been to protect the British community in case of trouble, and now the crisis was over. Captain Graham wrote to Commodore Hardy to explain the reason for the delay, while the *Doris* prepared for sea. There was a final burst of ceremonial on 12 October when the frigate and the other ships in the port marked the birthday of the Prince Regent of Brazil with gun salutes, followed by a dinner given by the British Consul. Then, on the 14th, *Doris* weighed anchor and headed down the coast for Bahia.

Situated in the centre of the eastern coast, Bahia was Brazil's most opulent and colourful province. It was a rolling fertile region, the source of an abundance of sugar, molasses, tobacco and cocoa, and the centre of a thriving trade in tropical produce and slaves through the magnificent baroque city of Salvador. Until the discovery of gold and diamonds had moved the centre of power southwards to Rio de Janeiro in the middle of the eighteenth century, Salvador de Bahia had been the seat of the viceroy and the centre of government. Built at the foot and up the slopes of a ridge on a peninsula commanding the eastern shore of a huge and magnificent bay, Salvador was still a busy commercial centre, its harbour thick with shipping, its wharves loaded with produce, its streets filled with bustling crowds. It was also a major military base and naval arsenal. And when constitutional fever hit the city, a strong Portuguese garrison was there to make sure there was no resistance from the Brazilians. They acted quickly to suppress any hostile murmuring and there were waves of arbitrary arrests. Nevertheless, *Doris* was to remain in Bahia for six weeks to reassure British merchants before it became clear that the security situation was well under control.

Three days after leaving Recife, *Doris* sighted Cape St Antonio at the eastern extremity of the Bay of Bahia, headed north for Salvador and, as darkness fell, dropped anchor off the port. Daylight crept over the Bay next morning, 17 October, to reveal what Maria Graham described as 'one of the finest scenes ever beheld' as she gazed at the tracery of the rigging of ships in the harbour, the white, red-roofed buildings of the city sweeping up the ridge and the lush green hills, dotted with convents and churches, melting into the distance. Meanwhile the frigate exchanged salutes with the island Fort do Mar guarding the harbour, and moved closer in to anchor. The captain immediately went on his official calls. Mrs Graham was not far behind. Met by Mr Consul Pennell, she landed at the dockyard – admiring the handsome frigate that was growing in the stocks[8] – then walked through the gate into the lower town. The place was filled with people – blacks in gaudy clothing with loads on their heads; vendors selling sausages, fried fish and sugar cakes; goldsmiths, jewellers and haberdashers at work in their shops. The narrow streets were filthy and difficult for wheeled traffic at the best of times. Now that the rainy season had arrived, they were impassable, so the party had to take the local form of a sedan chair to climb up to the upper town where the Pennells had their residence.

The Consul and his wife declared open house for the officers and midshipmen of the *Doris*, and there were numerous excursions into the countryside and to the Island of Itaparica across the Bay. Master Thomas Biddle with Midshipmen William Glennie and Frederick Grey went off in the pinnace with blankets and food for a five-day excursion to see Cachoeira at the inland extremity of the Bay, while Mrs Graham and the others enjoyed the pleasures of the city. They worshipped at the English church, heartily joining the Reverend Mr Synge in his prayer for 'Dom John of Portugal, Sovereign of these realms by whose gracious permission we are enabled to worship God according to our consciences'. There was also a visit to the opera to see a version of Voltaire's *Mohamed*. The performance was mediocre but no-one seemed to mind as the Portuguese ladies and gentlemen present were more concerned with talking, laughing, eating sweetmeats and drinking coffee than watching what was going on. The only disagreeable incident was that one of the midshipmen had his sword stolen, apparently by a local military officer in the next box.

Maria Graham also had her first experience of a Portuguese home. She joined happily in the conversation of the local ladies, and was interested to find that the favourite topic of discussion was the beauty of Bahia and its inhabitants, followed by clothes, children and diseases in that order. She noted that the womenfolk did not make themselves presentable until noon, and remarked on their general slovenliness, their greasy, unkempt hair and the scantiness of their clothing. Meeting the same ladies – now unrecognizably elegant and bejewelled – a few days later at a party given by the Consul, she reflected smugly that 'she who would be a gentlewoman in public must be one in private',[9] and noted with satisfaction the superior appearance of the more simply dressed English. Not that they came in for unalloyed praise. British society, she thought, was at a 'very low scale'. Hospitable and kind though they were, the men were preoccupied with business during the day and with food and gambling at night, and neither they nor their wives showed any curiosity about the country and society in which they lived, being unable even to name the fascinating plants that grew in such profusion round their doors.

There were more visits to the town to see the hospital, the female orphan asylum, the cathedral, the convents, the British mercantile establishments (there were 18 in Salvador, all trading with Liverpool) and – compulsory for all British visitors – the fascinating horror of the slave market. Mrs Graham discovered that no fewer than 76 slave ships had sailed from the port in the previous year, losing at least one-fifth of their cargoes on the return voyage. On 22 October they even had the opportunity to watch aghast as a slaver unloaded its pitiful cargo. HMS *Morgiana* of the West African anti-slavery patrol also arrived during the visit, and Captain Finlayson was able to regale them with horrific details of the trade, and with stories of slaves being thrown overboard during a chase.[10] There was a nasty incident when one of Finlayson's men was murdered ashore. It proved impossible to find the culprit, partly because of the notorious inefficiency of the police and partly because the *Morgiana* was highly unpopular locally as a result of her interception of Brazilian slave ships.

Meanwhile *Doris* was overhauled after her transatlantic crossing and prepared for the next leg of her voyage. As usual, fresh meat and provisions arrived alongside daily, while the men unreeved the ship's running rigging, loosed the sails to dry them, restored the paintwork to a pristine white and black, scrubbed hammocks and aired the lower decks.[11] There was also some coming and going among ships in the anchorage. As well as the *Morgiana*, other interesting ships had arrived – the packet *Wellington*, the Portuguese frigate *Dom Pedro*, and the French warship *Antigone*, where they met Captain Villeneuve, nephew of the French commander at Trafalgar. In her journal, Mrs Graham reflected that 'whenever France and England are not at war, the French and the English certainly seek each other out and like each other more than any other two nations ... and whenever we meet a Frenchman in time of peace in a distant country, it is something akin to the pleasure of seeing a countryman'.[12] Other people serving with the South America Squadron were not so sure. Midshipman Charles Drinkwater of the *Superb*, describing a party in Montevideo between officers of the British flagship and those of *Colosse* and *Galathée*, commented that the French were 'fine fellows, but after dinner when the wine began to flow pretty freely, they turned out to be regular Napoleon's men!' Hardy shared his scepticism and tactfully moved his ship down river to Maldonado to avoid any friction between his crews and those of the French.[13]

But there was also the harsher side of the frigate's visit to Bahia. On 1 November four men were flogged for disobedience and insolence. And a fortnight later the gratings were rigged once more, and six deserters who had been rounded up by Midshipman Turner were given 96 lashes each.[14] Another three had managed to get away, but their places were easily filled by volunteers from British seamen in the port.[15] Mrs Graham – who fortunately missed the grizzly spectacle by being away with the Pennells at the time – reported that they had been tempted away by an unscrupulous crimp who then made money by reporting their whereabouts to the authorities. Whatever the reason, *Doris* moved her anchorage to prevent more men swimming ashore.

The frigate was now ready to go. And not before time, for the heat and humidity of the Brazilian summer was making itself felt on the health of the crew. Captain Graham himself was ill, and an increasing number of the young gentlemen were going down with heatstroke or fever. There was even a death among the ship's company – 30-year-old William Kyle from Leith, a member of the carpenter's crew. Then on 8 December, Mrs Graham and the officers having said goodbye to new friends ashore, *Doris* weighed anchor and sailed out of the Bay of Bahia bound for the Brazilian capital of Rio de Janeiro.

CHAPTER 8

RIO DE JANEIRO AND ROUND CAPE HORN

On the afternoon of 14 December 1821 His Majesty's Ship *Doris* sighted the rocky promontory of Cape Frio, the landfall for all ships heading for Rio de Janeiro, headed west along the fringe of coastal mountains and dropped anchor as night fell off the entrance to the Bay of Guanabara. Next morning, with a following sea breeze, the frigate passed between the Sugar Loaf and the Fort of Santa Cruz and entered the blue sheltered waters of an enormous bay. On either side, a backdrop of spectacular mountain ranges opened up, dominated by the crooked peak of the Corcovado, or 'Lord Hood's nose' as British sailors liked to call it. In the foreground she passed wooded islands, bays and promontories, green banks and rocky outcrops crowned with white churches or forts until, coming abreast of the fortified island of Villegagnon, the city of Rio de Janeiro came into sight on the left, shimmering in the summer heat. *Doris* passed though a multitude of shipping, smartly took in sail and dropped anchor off the island of Ratos near the naval arsenal.

To the Grahams's disappointment, there was no sign of the South America Squadron's *Owen Glendower*, commanded by their friend the Hon. Robert Spencer. However, the brig *Beaver* was in Rio, and her captain was immediately rowed over to deliver letters which *Owen Glendower* had left before sailing for home. One was from Captain Spencer sending personal greetings and a useful Spanish dictionary. Another was from Sir Thomas Hardy, ordering *Doris* to pass round the Horn and to join him in the Pacific in the New Year if the situation in Brazil allowed it.

The political situation in Rio was approaching a crisis at that time, and it was three months before it was tranquil enough for Captain Graham to be able to leave Brazilian waters. The problem was that as soon as the King had returned to Portugal, the Côrtes tried to turn the clock back 15 years. The individual Brazilian provinces were made directly responsible to Lisbon once more, the government installations in Rio de Janeiro were abolished, and there were threats to restore the old commercial restrictions. Portuguese officials and merchants supported the changes, but Brazilians were shocked and angry at the obvious attempt to make their country a colonial appendage once more. Prince Regent Pedro, caught in the middle, vacillated between obedience to the Côrtes and defiance.

Then news arrived that Pedro too had been ordered back to Lisbon 'to complete his political education'. To Brazilian patriots, news of the Prince's recall came as final proof of the hostility of Portuguese intentions. Resolutions denouncing the Côrtes and begging the Prince to remain flooded in from the Brazilian provincial juntas. Pedro hesitated, then on 9 January 1822 threw his weight behind the Brazilian cause with the historic declaration that he intended to remain. Events moved rapidly. In an attempt to force the Prince to obey, Portuguese General Avilez de Souza Tavares, at the head of the Rio garrison, occupied the hill that dominated the city. Pedro immediately mobilized the Brazilian militia and, with a mixture of threats and personality, overawed the unhappy Avilez and made him and his men withdraw harmlessly across the Bay away from the deserted and apprehensive city.

Doris arrived in the middle of this drama, standing ready to protect an increasingly panicky British community. On 13 January arrangements were actually made for her to receive the Prince Regent and his family on board in case they needed refuge.[1] They did not. A month later the unhappy General Avilez submitted, and was sent back to Portugal with all his men, leaving Rio and central Brazil safely under Brazilian control. The Brazilians rejoiced, and *Doris* returned to the familiar routine. In addition to the normal tasks of painting ship, refurbishing the rigging and drying the sails, there were additional tasks necessary in the tropics. Melted tar and pitch in the sun-baked rigging and deck seams had to be restored, boats had to be recaulked and, to keep the ship healthy, the lower decks and orlop had to be regularly aired and washed, sprinkled with vinegar and occasionally whitewashed.[2]

The frigate had reached Brazil at the hottest and most humid time of the year, and the impact of the climate and the mosquitoes was making itself felt. Some of the youngsters were ailing – Midshipman Langford and First-Class Volunteer Boxald being badly ill – and Captain Graham himself was suffering from intermittent bouts of poor health. Most of the crew were able to recover, but on arrival in Rio, Boatswain Bond and 13 seamen had to be invalided ashore to await transport back to England. Another four, thrilled by the bright lights of Rio, promptly deserted. And there were two tragedies when a seaman fell to his death from the mizzentop and the Captain of the Mast died of natural causes. Once again there was no difficulty in finding seven volunteer British sailors to take their places.[3]

Maria Graham escaped the oppressive heat by moving into a house ashore located in a leafy valley at the foot of Corcovado called Laranjeiras after the orange trees that grew there in such abundance. Accompanied by Midshipman Langford and the other invalids, she walked and rode in the verdant countryside, enjoying the spectacular tropical scenery, the little coffee plantations, the thickets of flowering shrubs mingled with lemon blossom and jasmine, and the abundance of brilliant birds and huge armoured beetles. On their excursions they even met an old soldier, General Count Hogendorp, who had begun his career with Frederick the Great and had ended it serving Napoleon, and were invited to picnic on his veranda. Then there were visits to Rio's famous Botanical Garden and to the farms and courtyarded villas of British friends, including merchant William May – an old acquaintance – and Mr and Miss Haynes, the Slave Trade Commissioner and his sister.[4]

A week later Mrs Graham and Midshipman Glennie went to the town for the first time. They admired the great double-arched aqueduct carrying water to the city's four fountains, the dazzling white Gloria church on its wooded hill on the edge of the bay, the

**9 The entrance to Rio de Janeiro.
Engraving from *The Naval Chronicle***

10 View of Rio de Janeiro by Rugendas

gilded Chapel Royal with its library, the tall European-looking houses in the narrow streets, and the main square flanked on three sides by the Royal Palace and private houses, and on the fourth by a wide granite jetty with steps leading down to the water. But above all they enjoyed the commercial bustle in the streets, the cheerful-looking free blacks plying their trades, the gaily clad washerwomen at the fountains, the goldsmiths and artisans working in their shops, and the great number of British stores selling saddlery, cottons, crockery and every form of hardware. The whole waterfront area had a distinctive British air and Mrs Graham noted that there were as many '"Union Jacks", "Red Lions" and "Jolly Tars" as in Deptford or Greenwich'.[5] Then there were balls and parties, ashore and afloat. Captain Graham threw one on the *Doris*, clearing the decks, hiding the cannon behind screens, rigging canvas awnings and decorating the ship with flags, flowers and evergreens. It was a great success. Music was provided by musicians from the Opera House and the guests were both English and Brazilian, the latter led by a new friend, the Viscondessa do Rio Seco. Mrs Graham noted with approval that the local ladies were of a better class and decidedly superior to those in Bahia. As for those of the British community, 'very good persons doubtless' she confided in her journal, 'but it would require the pen of Miss Austen to make them interesting'.[6] More exciting were visits to the Opera – not because of the performance, but because the gala coincided with the height of the political crisis. Mrs Graham and the officers of the *Doris* were able to see the Prince and Princess in full dress in their box, and to witness the scenes of patriotic enthusiasm, the repeated renditions of the national anthem and the wild applause.

On 20 January 1822 HMS *Aurora* arrived. Her captain, Henry Prescott, was senior to Thomas Graham by one year, so took command in Hardy's absence. He decided that before sailing to Chile, *Doris* should take another look at the situation in Bahia. The round trip took five weeks, and provided the opportunity to enjoy a breath of fresh air and get down to some exercises with the great guns and the small arms. But the situation in Bahia was calm, and the frigate was back on 23 February.

For Mrs Graham, Lieutenant Dance and the midshipmen there was a final excursion into the countryside to escape the deadening heat of Rio de Janeiro. Boarding an intriguing local craft in which the black crew handled their oars standing and facing forwards, they travelled 12 miles further up the Bay to a small settlement of Nossa Senhora da Luz. There, staying in a white colonnaded mansion set amid lush green gardens and flowering shrubs, they were able to sample the exotic local fruits and to ride through fields of sugar cane, groves of orange and guavas, and pasturelands with grazing sheep and dun-coloured cattle. They were also able to witness the more agreeable side of a slave plantation – for such it was – at first hand. Mrs Graham attended the weekly muster of all the negroes on the estate, watched as they received their rations of farinha flour, kidney beans, dried beef and snuff, and attended an evening party in the workers' quarters, marvelling at their high spirits and the African instruments and rhythms to which they danced. Next day she accompanied the English supervisor on a tour of the fazenda, visiting the huts of slaves who were no longer able to work, passing the time of day with the workers and enquiring about their families – to all the world like a benevolent country squire visiting his tenants. Meanwhile the young men went on a shooting expedition in the marshes, returning with a bag of snipe, a pelican they were keen to stuff and a live monitor lizard.

Four days later they were back in Rio de Janeiro, greeting old naval friends as the *Superb* arrived from Valparaiso and the *Slaney* put in on her way home to England via Pernambuco. Most of the sick had recovered by this time, but 14-year-old Volunteer Boxald was still ill, so he was transferred to the sloop, together with 11 invalids from the *Aurora*, for the voyage to England.[7] *Slaney* carried a second member of the *Doris*'s crew in the shape of the Reverend Mr Penny. The Chaplain had liked the look of Recife, and when he was offered a post there with the local English church, he jumped at the chance.[8] For the remaining three years of the frigate's commission, the ship's company would have to do without professional religious guidance.

The arrival of a French frigate, corvette and brig in Rio also provided a novelty. The captain was incapacitated by regular attacks of gout and was unable to call on Commodore Roussin, but Mrs Graham visited the *Amazone* with Captain Prescott and some of *Doris*'s officers and, once more, was favourably impressed with the smartness of the ship and the gentlemanly demeanour and professionalism of the Frenchmen. But more impressive still was the oven that the *Amazone* carried in her lower deck. Not only did it ensure a regular supply of fresh bread and baguettes, but served to dry the whole ship.[9] The British glumly compared it with their own galley under the forecastle, which could do little more than boil cauldrons of meat, peas and duff.

Preparations for rounding the Horn were almost complete. The normal daily supply of fresh meat and vegetables was augmented by additional supplies of bread, meat and rum, and the water was topped up to 110 tons.[10] A handful of passengers also came on board to be delivered to Valparaiso. One was a small solemn boy called Vincente, son of the Chilean notable Felipe de Solar. Finally, on 9 March 1822, *Doris* was ready. The frigate weighed anchor, dipped her ensign in salute to the Fort of Santa Cruz, passed under the lee of the Sugar Loaf and sailed out of the Bay to be confronted by an impressive sight. There at anchor were the 74-gun Portuguese warship, *Dom João VI*, three frigates, two corvettes, a brig and a dozen transports carrying a replacement garrison for Rio de Janeiro. It looked as if the Côrtes was getting tough. But the Brazilian Government was not overawed. The ships were allowed to enter the Bay but were made to anchor under the guns of the fortifications. No-one was allowed to disembark or communicate with the shore until they had sworn obedience to the Prince Regent. Then, on 23 March, the whole squadron was ignominiously sent back to Portugal. But none of this was of much concern to HMS *Doris*. By that time she was east of the Falkland Islands and well on her way to Chile.

Doris had left Rio de Janeiro at the height of summer, with the thermometer standing at 92°F in the harbour. The heat and humidity had inevitably taken their toll in terms of an extensive sick list that included Captain Graham and Midshipman Blatchley. But as the voyage progressed, the situation steadily improved. After a week, the frigate was 700 miles south of Rio de Janeiro, to the east of the River Plate, with the thermometer showing 68°F. The invalids began to feel better. But the easterly breezes that had sped *Doris* comfortably on her way since leaving Rio de Janeiro now turned into gales. With the wind hard on her port quarter, the frigate plunged forward over a grey sea, her man-of-war pennant stiff as a board, able to carry nothing more than heavily reefed courses and a jib. Even so, on 16 March, she logged a run of 205 miles.[11]

In the weeks that followed, the wind moderated and veered to the south-west. Now thrashing along close hauled on the starboard tack under a thick grey sky, *Doris* headed due south as she was forced to the east of her destination. The temperature continued to drop. The crew were given gloves and canvas coats lined with felt to keep out the cold, the lower halves of the gun ports were caulked, deadlights were fitted over the windows, and extra preventer stays rigged to give extra strength to the masts.[12] Thoughts of teaching and of normal meals were abandoned as the violent motion of the ship upset possessions and equipment, and deposited books and food in the scuppers. Outside, the ship acquired a permanent escort of stormy petrels and the occasional albatross as she pitched and rolled over the cold green sea. Inside, portable stoves were tried to bring some warmth to the freezing lower decks, the officers no doubt remembering with envy the oven in the bowels of the *Amazone*, and a fire was kept alight in the fore cabin. It soon became the rendezvous for the midshipmen, the growing number of invalids and for little Vincente de Solar whom Maria Graham had taken under her wing.

On 24 March *Doris* was to the east of the Falkland Islands, still plunging south under a heavy grey sky. A week later a shift in the wind to the south enabled the frigate to head south-west towards Staten Island and the Horn. The thermometer went down to 41°F then to 32°F. There were flurries of snow and sleet. The rigging was encased in ice, and the ropes and canvas were frozen. One man broke two ribs slipping on to the deck; another was taken ill at the wheel. With the shock of the intense cold coming so soon after the heat of Rio, the sick list began to lengthen. The First Lieutenant and Captain Graham were both ill, leaving the capable

11 Log entry of *Doris* for 9 April 1822
Public Record Office

William Dance in charge of the management of the ship. Then, on 1 April, the clouds suddenly lifted and the frigate found itself in broad sunlight shouldering her way through a deep blue sea with advancing lines of white-crested waves. After weeks under leaden skies, the sunny interlude was stimulating for everyone. There were penguins and porpoises to look at, and whales rising to the surface and blowing alongside. The young men managed to catch some petrels, fulmars and an albatross, eagerly skinning and dissecting the bird with the special apparatus Midshipman Glennie had brought with him for the purpose.[13]

But it was only a lull, and the weather closed in once more. There were strong westerly winds that brought rain, snow and sleet, forcing *Doris* further and further south and preventing her from turning west into the Pacific. On 8 April, at 60°14'S, 70°20'W – 150 miles south of Cape Horn and still heading south-west under close-reefed foresail and topsails – the weather suddenly brightened and they sighted a cliff of ice, estimated to be 410 feet high. There was a lively debate about whether it was an iceberg or the coast of the newly discovered South Shetlands.[14] The islands had been located two years earlier by Edward Bransfield, Master of HMS *Andromache*, who had been sent south by Captain Shirreff in the hired brig *Williams* for the purpose. When the discussion turned from exploration to the wreck of a Spanish warship that had been found on the islands, little Vincente's dark eyes had lit up and he had piped 'Mirad la Fortuna de Chile. When the tyrants send ships to oppress her, God sends them to wreck on desert coasts!'[15]

The morning was moderate and bright enough to enable the crew to dry their wet clothes, but the weather closed in during the afternoon with heavy seas, a grey overcast sky and sleet. But that night came a tragedy. The Captain had been ill since the *Doris* had left Rio de Janeiro. As the frigate had pushed further and further south, his condition had deteriorated until at the beginning of April he suffered a stroke. Mrs Graham sat up with her husband for nights at a stretch, but there was nothing that she, nor Surgeon Louden and his assistant Arthur Kift who were also in constant attendance, could do for the sick man. The bitter cold, the damp,

and the motion of the ship took their toll until, in the early hours
of 9 April 1822, Captain Graham died.

CHAPTER 9

TRAVELS IN CHILE
AND PERU

On 26 April 1822, after 48 days at sea, HMS *Doris* at last sighted
the brilliant line of white peaks that marked the Chilean cordillera,
and headed up the coast for Valparaiso. Two days later she entered
the semi-circular bay on which the city was built, exchanged
salutes with the fort at its southern extremity, and dropped anchor
in the harbour. The roadstead was thick with merchant shipping
and naval vessels, both Chilean and foreign. Among the latter were
HMS *Blossom* of the South American Squadron, and two United
States ships, the big 74-gun *Franklin* and the frigate *Constellation*.
The sight of the *Doris* approaching with colours at half mast
caused an immediate stir, which changed to shock when the reason
became known. The American Commodore and Mrs Stewart went
on board the frigate to offer Maria Graham sympathy and a
passage back to Rio on the *Constellation* – due to return to the USA
next morning – should she desire it. But she felt mentally and
physically unable to face the return voyage at such a time and
declined, deciding to try her luck in Chile. Next day the Stewarts
returned, accompanied this time by the American Consul Mr
Hogan, his wife and daughter, who were to provide help and
comfort in the months that followed. Another visitor to the *Doris*
was Captain Vernon of the *Blossom*. But his mission was less
delicate. He had come to take command.

The next day, Captain Graham's body was rowed ashore and
given a military funeral arranged by the Chilean authorities in the
local citadel, attended by officers and men from all the British,
American and Chilean ships in the harbour, their flags hanging at

half mast. It was a melancholy and moving moment for Mrs Graham, made all the more poignant by the fact that one of the ships she could see at anchor was the Chilean brig *Galvarino* which, in a previous existence, had been HMS *Hecate*, her husband's first command. Then, with the ceremony over and the officers and men marching with their bands back to the ships, the widow moved into a cottage on the outskirts of Valparaiso to begin a new phase of her life.

HMS *Doris* too was about to begin a new phase. Her captain was now the 32-year-old Frederick Edward Venables Vernon, a veteran of the Napoleonic Wars where he had served in the West Indies, the Baltic and on the coasts of Spain and France. Vernon was a son of the Archbishop of York, a grandson of the Marquis of Stafford, and was related by marriage to no less than five earls.[1] He had had sufficient political pull to obtain promotion to post captain at the age of 24, but his position on the fringe of the aristocracy as the fifth of nine children seemed to make him uncertain, and he was as ingratiating and anxious to please his superiors as he was strict with his subordinates. As a commander he was precise and fussy, perhaps showing the same family characteristics that qualified so many of his relations for high positions in the Church and the universities. In the squadron he was regarded as a rather colourless figure.[2] Captain Vernon's arrival caused other changes in the frigate. As was the custom, he brought his 'followers' with him – 17 in all, including his steward, coxswain and cook, and Midshipmen Anson, Lloyd and Milner. In return, 15 of *Doris*'s men moved to *Blossom*. Among them were Midshipmen Fitzmaurice and Brisbane, and Lieutenant James Henderson who was to be acting captain.[3] Henderson knew that this was likely to be his last opportunity of achieving promotion and wrote immediately to the Admiralty enforcing his claims to be confirmed as a captain or, at least, a commander. He had – as he pointed out – 26 years of experience, had served as a first lieutenant on frigates since 1809, and had now been left in command of a ship due to the death of his captain on no less than two occasions.[4]

Doris had missed Sir Thomas Hardy by three weeks. On the

orders of the Admiralty, who regarded the struggle in the Pacific as good as over and saw Brazil as the next area of crisis, the Commodore had sailed for Rio de Janeiro in *Creole* on 28 March 1822. But he had left letters and secret instructions[5] stressing the need to protect British interests and to observe strict neutrality in the conflict. *Doris* was the only British ship of force on the station at the time. *Conway* had been ordered to go north as far as Panama but to return to Peru and Chile by 1 May,[6] but there was no sign of her. Hardy generously explained to the Admiralty that he had 'no doubt that Captain Hall had found himself imperiously called upon to exceed his orders in remaining so far northwards'.[7] At that moment Hall was actually loading $700,000 (£140,000) in bullion for transportation to England on behalf of British merchants in San Blas, in what is now Ecuador, and was keenly awaiting a second instalment. And when the loading had finished in the middle of June, Hall yielded to the persuasion of the local merchants, ignored his orders and made straight for Brazil round Cape Horn without calling at either Peru or Chile.[8]

With ugly rumours of the state of affairs in Peru now regularly arriving in Valparaiso, Captain Vernon was keen to be off. But for once the Navy's victualling arrangement hit a snag. There was plenty of rum, vinegar, sugar and beef – including a dozen live bullocks – but *Doris* was stuck in Valparaiso for a month by a shortage of bread.[9] The officers used the opportunity to enjoy the fresh late summer air, to shoot partridges in the marshes, and to see the sights. Valparaiso was a long straggling town built round the bay between the cliffs and the sea, its low whitewashed, red-tiled houses spreading up a number of short ravines and across a flat plain to the east. Clustered in the port area were churches, fish and meat markets and numerous bustling shops offering a variety of international wares. There was flour and furniture from the USA, silks and millinery from France, glass and knick-knacks from Germany and – dominating everything – cottons, woollens, hardware and crockery from Britain. The town was thick with the signs of English saddlers, shoemakers, tailors and inn keepers, and the officers learnt with astonishment that one of the most popular of English imports was pianos. Almost every house, they were told, had one. The men liked the place as well and five deserted. One – Able Seaman Silas Pinnock – was soon caught, and the rest were, as usual, easily replaced by local British volunteers.[10] But on 20 May the frigate's provisioning was at last complete – 21,000 lbs of bread had been found, and *Doris* sailed to keep an eye on things in Callao, the port of Lima.

The great Chilean expedition of 1820 against Peru had been successful – up to a point. General San Martin, anxious to preserve his only army intact and confident that the confusion on the royalist side would cause Lima to fall into his hands like a ripe plum, had proceeded cautiously. And by August 1821 the royalists had withdrawn into the interior, Peru had declared its independence, and San Martin had been proclaimed Protector. The impatient Lord Cochrane was typically insensitive to San Martin's reasoning and was openly critical of his strategy, favouring a head-on attack, and when the Protector began to recruit Chilean officers and seamen into the service of Peru – refusing to offer them any pay unless they did so – he was furious. Cochrane flatly rejected San Martin's offer to take command of the new Peruvian Navy himself, and watched impotently as 15 disenchanted sea officers, led by his most senior captains, Guise, Spry, Esmonde, Carter and Prunier, took up appointments in the new force. In September he seized a ship loaded with treasure belonging to San Martin, which he used to pay his remaining men. He then disappeared north in pursuit of the only remaining representatives of Spanish sea power in the Pacific, the *Prueba* and *Venganza*. Unfortunately for him, both frigates ran short of supplies and, lacking any kind of base, had no alternative but to surrender to the Peruvian authorities in Guayaquil early in 1822. His temper not improved by this loss of prize money, Cochrane returned to Callao in May for a final spate of quarrelling with San Martin, then led the remnants of his squadron back to Chile.

Captain Vernon and *Doris* arrived at Callao in early June, relieving the 10-gun brig *Alacrity* which returned to Valparaiso carrying a useful freight of $650,000 (£160,250) on behalf of local British merchants.[11] A royalist army was still at large in the interior of the country, but the coast was now peaceful and under Peruvian patriot control. There was therefore little for the British frigate to do but report on the occasional military excursion against the royalists, and to observe the increasingly oppressive actions of San Martin's agents against old Spaniards and, indeed, anyone the regime disliked or envied. Nevertheless, with both new republics now possessing navies, Hardy felt that a force of at least three Royal Naval vessels was necessary on the Pacific coast,[12] two to keep watch on Callao and Valparaiso, the third to visit the northern ports as far as Acapulco. The Americans and the French were taking similar precautions and, in August, *Doris* was joined by the USS *Franklin* and the *Clorinde*.

Doris spent three long months in Callao. There was plenty of time to refurbish the frigate's sails and fabric after the long voyage round the Horn from Rio. The lower decks were scoured and recaulked, the running rigging overhauled, the yards blackened, the iron work repaired and the ship repainted. And there were plenty of men to do it. Ten British seamen from the port reported as volunteers during June, and *Doris* was able to exchange small groups of men with the crews of HMS *Alacrity*, the whaler *Adventure* and the merchant brig *Importer*. There were only two desertions, Able Seamen William Small and Jonathan Steel who had volunteered less than two months before.

Her refurbishment complete, the normal routine of a warship took over. There was fresh beef, fresh vegetables and grog daily, divine service on Sundays, the twice-weekly scrubbing of hammocks and clothes on Tuesday and Friday, and the regular cleansing of the lower decks on Saturdays. Meanwhile Captain Vernon energetically began to put the stamp of his personality on the ship. There were now twice-weekly exercises of the great guns and of the small arms men and Royal Marines. Vernon clearly believed that a ship-of-war should be in a high state of readiness and, on at least two occasions ordered the guns to be loaded with ball as well as powder and fired at a target. Unfortunately the Ordnance Board took a different view, and Vernon was dismayed to find on his return to England that he had been surcharged £6 13s 4d for what it regarded as an unnecessary waste of shot.[13]

There was also a sharp increase in the use of the lash. With

Vernon in command of *Doris*, the monthly average went up to eight floggings and 165 lashes. The most common offence was now drunkenness, possibly brought on by the tedium of life at Callao. Only when the *Aurora* arrived on 27 July carrying Commodore Hardy's reprimand for the excessive punishments on *Doris* did they suddenly fall. For the following year, Vernon's monthly average went down to three floggings and 66 lashes. The same number of men were flogged in this period as in Captain Graham's time, but they received half as many lashes. The reasons varied from insolence (34 per cent) and drunkenness (40 per cent) to neglect of duty, fighting and theft (4 per cent each).[14]

With the situation on the Pacific coast apparently under control, Captain Prescott as senior naval officer decided to order *Doris* back to Valparaiso, then round the Horn to join Commodore Hardy in Brazil. Accordingly, on 23 August, the frigate's crew weighed anchor, made sail and thankfully left the port of Callao, heading south for Chile. After a squally passage, they arrived three weeks later on 14 September to find the *Alacrity* and the disconsolate remnants of the Chilean squadron – the *O'Higgins, Independencia, Valdavia, Galvarino* and *Montezuma* – riding at their anchors in the bay. The country was at peace, but the navy was rent by a furious dispute between Cochrane and the Chilean authorities over the non-payment of his men. Then, in October, news arrived from Peru that a sovereign congress had assumed power and that a disillusioned San Martin had decided to retire from the scene. A week later the information was confirmed by the arrival of the long-faced, lugubrious General himself, explaining that he wished to bathe his rheumatic arm at a well-known Chilean spa before making his way to Europe. Captain Spencer of *Alacrity* immediately posted overland across the Andes to the River Plate with the news, while his ship promptly transferred its freight of bullion to the *Doris*[15] in iron chests and headed for Callao to reinforce the *Aurora*.

San Martin's arrival in Chile caused a problem, but whatever tensions had developed between the two states, no-one could forget his crucial contribution over many years to the independence of South America. The General was treated with respect and courtesy. Only Lord Cochrane, insensitive and petulant as ever, not only suggested publicly that there should be an enquiry into San Martin's disloyalty, his attempts to seduce its navy, and 'other demonstrations and acts of hostility towards the Republic of Chile', but offered to be the principal witness for the prosecution. The Chileans tactfully ignored him.

The attitude of the British community towards Cochrane and his innumerable quarrels was divided. In their many memoirs, long-term adherents of the regime tended to be unfavourable, while short-term residents and visitors (like Maria Graham who got to know him and his captains well during her stay) came down strongly in his favour. Royal Navy officers were equally divided, as was exemplified by the different attitudes of Captains Searle and Shirreff. What the lower deck thought is generally unknown, but the humble crippled clerk of the *Owen Glendower*, Thomas Collings, whose own expectation of growing wealthy on prize money was small, was certainly critical. In his private journal he compared Cochrane unfavourably with the heroic and disinterested patriot San Martin, describing him as a man whose military accomplishments might be brilliant, but whose hand 'was always stretched out and whose lips were constantly uttering the cry "Silver, give me silver"'.[16]

While in Valparaiso Cochrane's detractors played on his reputation for financial gain to spread rumours that, while the Chilean Navy went unpaid, the Admiral was feathering his own nest by shipping two crates containing 18,000 ounces of gold dust and silver bars to England aboard HMS *Doris*. His closest 'followers', Captains Cobbett, Crosbie and Wilkinson, went aboard the frigate to establish the falsity of the story; then warned Cochrane, who hastily returned from his estate at Quinteiro to defend his reputation.

Doris was in Valparaiso for one month, completing preparations for the return voyage round the Horn. With the hull now in good repair, the crew concentrated on the standing and running rigging under the direction of Boatswain Peterson, who had come from *Blossom* with Captain Vernon. At the same time, the frigate replenished its supply of naval stores, in the form of canvas, nails, rope, and barrels of tallow, tar and varnish. There were also

British-made blankets and slop clothing to be loaded – bales containing monkey jackets, shirts, sailors' frocks, and blue cloth coats. On the provisioning side there was, as before, a shortage of bread and Purser Worth was only able to find 6600 lbs – a month's supply – in place of the 24,000 lbs he had been ordered to find. But there was plenty of rum, wine, vinegar, tobacco, pork and beef – both in the cask and on the hoof. Captain Vernon also discovered that cocoa was readily available and was going cheap. In the national interest he therefore loaded 14,975 lbs – an enormous quantity that was to keep the South America Squadron going for a year.[17]

The delights of Valparaiso also triggered the usual trickle of deserters – this time, William Ward, a Londoner who had never previously been in trouble, and Silas Pinnock from Shaftesbury who had been flogged for attempted desertion in Bahia, fined £3 for a second attempt, and who now managed to get away at the third. But unusually, the volunteers who filled their places were natives of Tahiti, called Arape and Aotaere. Equally unusual was the fact that both had enough seagoing experience to be rated as ordinary seamen.

For the officers and midshipmen of the *Doris*, the return to Valparaiso provided a welcome chance to see their old friend Mrs Graham once more. Many had written regularly to her from Callao. But Maria was not at home. She had decided to visit the Chilean capital of Santiago, and a month earlier had set out on horseback up the new carriage road into the mountains, accompanied by Midshipman the Hon. Frederick de Roos of *Alacrity* and by numerous peons and baggage mules. Thus when *Doris* arrived in Valparaiso, Maria was already enjoying the pleasures of the Chilean capital and the farms and *sitios* scattered around in the plain and foothills of the Andes. Accompanied by new friends in the shape of the families of American Consul General Judge Prevost and of two Chilean notables, José Antonio de Cotapos and Felipe de Solar (whose son, the precocious patriot Vincente, had travelled with her round the Horn) she was busy sketching, collecting materials and energetically visiting the mint, the Assembly, the printing office, the library, the cathedral and the theatre.

12 Maria Graham
Drawing by Charles Eastlake 1819.

She also had time to visit the convent of Saint Auguste, noting with good Protestant satisfaction that, although their maté-tea was excellent, the nuns were old and ugly and the institution was unlikely to survive. She also had numerous meetings with the Director of Chile, Bernardo O'Higgins – short, stout but dignified in general's uniform. They were able not only to discuss the state of South America but to exchange memories of Richmond where O'Higgins had gone to school and where Mrs Graham had spent a happy time at the house of an uncle.[18]

On 24 September Lieutenant Dance and Midshipman Candler of *Doris* suddenly appeared in Santiago carrying letters and greetings. They had been deputed by their colleagues to check on Mrs Graham's well being and bring her home. It was just as well they came. For Maria's exertions had proved too much and a fortnight previously she had fallen ill with a recurrence of her old consumption and was spitting blood. With the help of her Chilean friends, the two officers made all the arrangements for the return journey, managing to get hold of a local carriage lined with yellow silk but of robust construction with heavy axles and two crude red-painted wheels. Four days later Mrs Graham said farewell to her many friends, turned her back regretfully on the dazzling snow-capped peaks of the Chilean Cordillera and headed west down the carriage road to Valparaiso.

The journey took three days. On the first, the cavalcade – made up of Maria Graham's creaking carriage, Dance and Candler wearing Chilean costume including ponchos and huge silver spurs, and the accompanying peons and baggage mules – followed the long straight road through the sandy plain to the Lake of Pudajuel, then over the pass on the Cuesta de Prado with its thickets, giant thistles and occasional tall trees, and out the other side to a post-house where they spent the night. The second day took them down a series of long undulating valleys between the surrounding mountains, thick with grass and wild flowers and past scattered hamlets set among streams, blooming orchards and vines. Then they passed through woody glens and evergreens and up over the top of another ridge, the road then curving down the mountain in 16 serpentine loops, to the plain where lay their destination, the

tiny town of Casablanca. Boasting little more than a main street, a
church, a central plaza used for the annual bullfight, and a number
of inns, Casablanca was nevertheless the centre of an agricultural
area renowned for its dairy products, and provided good accommodation for travellers on the road. Next day Maria Graham's
party set out on the last leg of the journey, a straight 30-mile
stretch through a flat grassy, well-watered and treeless plain, thick
with herds of cattle, the road only deviating halfway to wind
through an area of grassy hills and shaded streams which the
travellers likened to Devonshire. Eventually they reached the last
post-house before Valparaiso, to be surprised by an enthusiastic
welcoming committee made up of Captain Spencer of *Alacrity* and
a group of the *Doris*'s midshipmen. One of them was Maria
Graham's cousin William Glennie, who had been invalided ashore
with what appeared to be the first signs of consumption, and was
to spend the next six months with her. There was a change of
horses and convivial refreshment. Then the cheerful party completed the last dozen miles to Valparaiso, following the broad
carriage road that wound down from the heights to the port.

But *Doris*'s departure was delayed for another fortnight. No
sooner had Lieutenant Dance's party returned, than it was Captain
Vernon's turn to post up the road to Santiago. There were stories
that new commercial regulations imposing higher duties on
imported manufactures were about to be introduced in spite of an
agreement that six months' notice would be given. The rumours
were correct. Captain Vernon lodged an official protest, but the
new rules seemed so contradictory and their purpose in protecting
local industries which hardly existed so pointless that no problem
was expected.[19]

In Vernon's absence, the officers of the *Doris* had been given a
final reshuffle. First, a disappointed Lieutenant Henderson
returned on board a merchant brig having relinquished his temporary command of the *Blossom*. Henderson lacked the 'interest' to be
confirmed as either a commander or a captain, which went on
promotion to Commander Archie Maclean of the *Beaver*. Then one
of *Doris*'s original lieutenants, John Smart, was posted to *Alacrity*
and was temporarily replaced by Lieutenant James MacDonald

who had travelled from Rio in a fruitless search for the *Conway*, his next posting. MacDonald was an experienced and imaginative officer. When first lieutenant of the *Owen Glendower* he had distinguished himself by decorating the lower deck in the manner of an English village. The bulwarks and side planking were painted red and white to look like bricks and mortar, the masts were covered in mottled grey to resemble marble columns, and the surgeon's chest was converted into a marble tomb with a suitable memorial inscription![20] Unfortunately, when transferred to *Alacrity* with her newly promoted captain, the Hon. Fred Spencer, he had foolishly put it about that he was being sent there to act as the young aristocrat's wet nurse. He had not therefore lasted long. His stay on *Doris* was also short, and on 14 October – after only three weeks – he became a passenger once more when James Anderson, also of *Alacrity* and one of Sir Thomas Hardy's 'followers', being an old midshipman from the American War, was promoted to the frigate as a lieutenant.

Doris now made her final preparations. Water was pumped aboard to give 108 tons and, to increase the frigate's stability on the voyage round Cape Horn, Captain Vernon ordered that all the upper deck guns should be removed and secured below. That done, on 16 October 1822 *Doris* weighed anchor and, driven by a strong following breeze, sailed out of Valparaiso Bay for Rio de Janeiro. In her hold were 'remittances' in silver and bullion worth £130,000. Of this amount, a modest £3400 belonging to Lord Cochrane had been put aboard four days before the frigate sailed.[21] *Doris* was not to reappear in the Pacific during this commission.

CHAPTER 10

THE STRUGGLE FOR BAHIA

The voyage round Cape Horn lasted a month. Then, on 18 November 1822, *Doris* sighted the dramatic serrated coastline of central Brazil once more, and by late afternoon had entered the Bay of Guanabara, passed the island of Villegagnon and dropped anchor in the glittering water before Rio de Janeiro. There among a throng of merchantmen and lateen-rigged coasters were two ships of the British South America Squadron – *Blossom* and the elusive *Conway* – and two French vessels, the frigate *Amazone* and the corvette *Pomoné*. Immediately the boom of *Doris*'s cannon began to reverberate round the Bay as she began to salute, exchanging 13 guns with the flagship of the recently promoted French Rear Admiral Roussin, and 21 guns with the forts guarding the anchorage. But the flag that floated in the blue skies over the city and the fortifications was no longer the white banner of Portugal. In its place was a green ensign bearing a yellow lozenge with a crowned armillary sphere. It was the flag of the newly declared Brazilian Empire.

Much had happened in Brazil in the ten months since Captain Graham had sailed with *Doris* for Cape Horn. The growing resentment between Brazilians and Portuguese had boiled over into open conflict. A new government, led by a tough 58-year-old Paulista patriot called José Bonifácio de Andrada e Silva, had defied the Côrtes, nullified its most objectionable decrees and reunited the Brazilian provinces under Rio de Janeiro. It had won the Prince Regent to the cause and in May, Pedro had accepted the title of 'Perpetual Defender and Protector of Brazil'. In reply, an angry Côrtes promptly ordered him to dismiss his government, arrest its leading figures and reverse its policies. And it was the delivery of these orders on 7 September 1822 that caused the most famous event in Brazilian history. The courier caught up with the Prince near the Ypiranga stream during a flying visit to São Paulo. Pedro read the papers, then, pale with fury and defiance, drew his sword and to the cheers of the escorting Brazilian dragoons cried 'The time has come! It is Independence or Death. We are separated from Portugal!' On 12 October 1822 – his 24th birthday – Pedro was proclaimed 'Constitutional Emperor' of Independent Brazil. And on 1 December 1822 he was crowned, wearing – as if to symbolize the European and American origins of the Brazilian revolution – a green gold-laced uniform, a cloak of red parrot feathers and cavalry boots.

To declare independence was one thing, to achieve it another. In September 1822 only the central region of Brazil based on Rio was under Pedro's control. In the deep south the occupying army had split on the independence issue, and the Portuguese regiments had shut themselves up in Montevideo where they were besieged by their erstwhile Brazilian comrades. In the north and the north-east, something similar happened. The countryside had rallied to the imperial cause led by a hotch-potch of Brazilian militia and army units, while Portuguese merchants and troops secured control of the larger towns and the provincial capitals. Only in Pernambuco, with its revolutionary traditions, was there universal support for independence. Governor Luis do Rego, who had been so friendly to *Doris* on her first visit, had long ago returned to Lisbon and had been replaced by a Brazilian 'patriot' junta.

But it was in Bahia, with its great naval arsenal and populous hinterland, that the issue was to be decided. The struggle began there in February 1822, when Portuguese troops under Brigadier Ignacio Madeira de Melo had taken bloody control of Salvador. Brazilian army units and officials had promptly abandoned the city to organize resistance in the countryside and, by the middle of the year, had secured complete control of the province. Soon a motley Brazilian army of 10,000 men advanced on the capital and put it under siege. An attempt to dislodge the Portuguese using a naval expedition ignominiously failed. Meanwhile Madeira de Melo fortified Salvador and waited confidently for reinforcements.

It was clear to the Brazilian Government from the beginning that the independence issue would be decided by sea power. Only by seizing control of the sea could Brazil halt the supply of Portuguese reinforcements, blockade their coastal garrisons, then expel the troops that controlled most of the provincial centres. José Bonifácio and his Minister of Marine had therefore thrown their energies into creating a new national navy. The nucleus was provided by half a dozen Portuguese warships that were seized in Rio de Janeiro, and by an old two-decker and a frigate which were refitting in the dockyard. Then, using funds raised by an enthusiastically supported national subscription, they scoured the region for vessels available for purchase, and ordered vast quantities of naval stores and munitions from London.

But Brazil's greatest problem was manpower. The number of junior and middle-ranking officers available for the new navy was woefully inadequate, and the mood of the largely Portuguese-born sailors was sullen if not openly mutinous. A recruiting campaign aimed at nationals proved a failure, and the government therefore fell back on the local enlistment of foreigners. The first recruit was Captain David Jewitt, an American officer with experience in the navy of Buenos Aires. The second was William Eyre, originally an Admiralty midshipman on *Conway* who had resigned his post to follow his fortune in Brazil. But then the net was broadened. Hearing of Lord Cochrane's difficulties in Chile and Peru, José Bonifácio sent the Admiral a dramatic invitation to join the imperial service and – with suitable remuneration – to lead the cause of liberty in Brazil. At the same time, the Brazilian Agent in England, General Felisberto Brant, was ordered to begin a secret recruiting campaign in London and Liverpool. He was spectacularly successful. By March 1823 450 British seamen and 45 officers, or aspirant officers, had signed on – many of them Royal Navy veterans – and were on their way to swell the ranks of the Brazilian Navy. It was the leadership of Cochrane and the experience and ability of these men that were eventually to prove decisive in the struggle.[1]

Dramatic events were taking place in the capital, but it was clear to Sir Thomas Hardy that the fate of Brazil would be decided in Bahia. He was also fully aware of the need to be there in order to protect British investments in the city, worth £1 million, and British goods valued at £300,000.[2] On 9 September 1822 Hardy therefore headed north in his new flagship, the 44-gun frigate *Creole*, now commanded by Captain the Hon. Frederick Spencer, enjoying his second promotion in two years. For the next nine months the Commodore made Salvador his base, reporting developments to the Admiralty, soothing the anxieties of panicking British merchants, and carefully deploying the ships of the British South America Squadron around the various trouble spots. He now had *Creole*, *Beaver* and *Doris* in Brazilian waters, *Blossom* in the River Plate, and *Aurora* and *Alacrity* in the Pacific. *Conway* should have been there too, and Hardy was not pleased to receive news of the sloop's arrival in Rio directly from San Blas without touching at Callao and Valparaiso. Captain Hall was sent a stern rebuke for having 'seriously discommoded my plans for the … protection of British property in Peru'.[3] But Hardy's displeasure did not stop him ensuring that Hall sailed for England carrying a substantial 'freight' in dollars, and on arrival in Rio de Janeiro one of *Doris*'s first tasks was to transfer the money she had carried round the Horn. It took the crew of the frigate three days to transfer the heavy boxes of coin and bullion to the *Conway*'s hold.[4]

Sir Thomas Hardy had left orders for *Doris* to join him in Bahia without delay, but first to load up with as many provisions as the frigate could carry. Salvador was beginning to feel the effects of the siege in terms of severe food shortages and soaring prices, and the British ships were being thrown back on their own resources rather than rely on supplies from the shore. Fortunately *Doris* had completed the trip round Cape Horn with minimum damage. It was only necessary to repair a sprung maintopmast and to scrape and caulk the decks which were already suffering in the heat of another Brazilian summer. But that done, Captain Vernon did as he was ordered. On 3 December *Doris* topped up her stores, taking on board 17,000 lbs of bread, 3648 lbs of beef, 1960 lbs of flour, 150 lbs of raisins, 2850 lbs of sugar, 1013 gallons of rum, 420 gallons of wine, 130 gallons of vinegar, 45 gallons of lime juice, and 20 live oxen of 300 lbs each together with their fodder.[5] On 5

13 Brazil 1823

December *Doris* was towed by her boats out of the airless heat of the Bay of Guanabara, dipped her ensign to the forts at the entrance, then, catching the sea breeze on her starboard beam, slowly headed east for Cape Frio and the sea routes to the north.

A week later, on a cloudy morning with flurries of rain, *Doris* reached the entrance to the Bay of Bahia, followed the eastern shore as far as the Fort do Mar, then turned and dropped anchor off the port of Salvador. There awaiting her arrival were HMS *Creole*, flying Sir Thomas Hardy's broad pennant, and the brig *Beaver*. *Conway*, which had sailed from Rio earlier, joined later in the day. Once more the salutes began – 17 for the Portuguese ensign on the fort and 15 for a Portuguese flag officer, for the reinforcements so eagerly awaited by Military Governor Madeira de Melo had begun to arrive. The city was now defended by 5000 troops and a powerful force of 12 naval vessels commanded by Commodore Felix Pereira de Campos, flying his flag in the 74-gun *Dom João VI*. Also busy fitting out for sea was the big frigate *Constituição*, which Maria Graham had so admired on the stocks 18 months before.

Doris's first task was to reprovision her consorts from the stores she had brought from Rio de Janeiro. For a week the frigate busied herself slaughtering bullocks and transferring bread, cocoa and fresh meat to *Creole* and *Beaver*. Then, on 17 December, Sir Thomas Hardy's pennant was struck from *Creole* and hoisted on *Doris*, which now became the temporary flagship of the South America Squadron. Although the Commodore visited the frigate twice to attend divine service and muster the crew, it was largely a token honour since he was living ashore in a spacious house with a yard for livestock which he had taken as his residence and headquarters. That done, *Creole* sailed south to keep an eye on things in Rio de Janeiro and to load more provisions.

The next task was to complete arrangements for *Conway*'s return to England after her three years in South American waters. Cables and ballast were moved between the ships, and final adjustments were made to personnel. Midshipmen Grey and Langford were transferred from *Doris* to *Conway* for the return voyage, and five seamen were exchanged. Captain Vernon cleverly ensured that they included one of the frigate's black sheep, Daniel McAuliffe. They were joined by 13 other men who were to be invalided home. One was Lieutenant Henderson, either genuinely sick or disappointed at the failure of his bid to secure promotion. Another was the ship's carpenter. Seven local volunteers were taken on to bring the frigate's crew up to strength, and deserter Able Seaman Robert Campbell who had been absent for a year was retaken. There were also three exchanges. Lieutenant Anderson went to *Beaver*, Midshipman Cunningham to *Creole*, and Midshipman Parry to *Blossom* with Volunteer Desauges. They were replaced by Lieutenant Frampton and by Midshipmen Noble and Fowke.[6] Even so, with Henderson's departure, *Doris* was an officer short. Commodore Hardy solved the problem by appointing Lieutenant John Taylor to the frigate from *Blossom*, sending him orders in Rio de Janeiro to travel to Bahia in *Creole* when she returned.

Conway and *Beaver* both sailed from Salvador on 2 January 1823, the first for England, the second for the River Plate via Rio de Janeiro. That done, Sir Thomas Hardy and *Doris* settled down to observe the progress of the siege. There was little to see in the way of action. Brazilian military pressure and a succession of rebuffs had sapped the morale of the defenders. Food was short, trade was at a standstill, and the city's finances were strained to breaking point. Madeira de Melo now commanded 5000 troops, but was only able to maintain the defence by using the seamen from the naval squadron which, to the anger of the population, was left almost idle at its anchorage. Hardy himself was surprised to see that Portuguese maritime strategy was entirely defensive, directed at carrying reinforcements or seeking supplies in spite of the fact that the squadron was 'looking remarkably well and formidable'.[7]

Doris was moored off Salvador for two months, sails dried and furled, canvas awnings rigged to protect her crew and decks from the burning sun and the occasional tropical downpour. As she swung languidly in the blue water, there was ample time to repaint the ship, tar the standing rigging and repair a strained foretopsail yard. Normal routine returned as Vernon wanted it – mustering and inspection of men and clothing, divine service on Sunday, the scrubbing of hammocks and the washing of clothes twice a week. As an extra precaution in the heat, the lower decks were washed and aired weekly and whitewashed once a month. When conditions permitted, there were exercises with the guns and small arms. There was little else to do. The *Doris*'s officers and men could admire the dramatic scenery of the Bay of Bahia and the sight of the city sweeping up the lush greenery of the ridge, but with Salvador now under siege, there were no more parties or balls ashore and no more expeditions into the countryside. The only breaks in routine were trips to the empty town or to the gates to watch the twice daily exodus of dejected refugees to the Brazilian lines.[8] Four seamen – Jonathan Flood, William Taylor, William Pelham and John Williams – relieved the monotony by abandoning their boat while it was watering and disappearing ashore. But with the city under siege there was nowhere to go, and they were rounded up a week later. In the circumstances, Captain Vernon decided that they were 'stragglers' rather than 'deserters' and decreed that £3 should be deducted from their pay as a punishment.

But Lieutenant Thomas Frampton was new and keen. He detected a suspicious increase in shore traffic, and on closer investigation became convinced that the Purser, Bartholomew Worth, and the Master, Thomas Biddle, were involved in a fraud. When the frigate had been in Callao the two men had bought and secreted aboard a quantity of cocoa. Now in Salvador they were in the process of smuggling the sacks ashore and selling them at inflated 'siege' prices through a local merchant called Power. When challenged by Captain Vernon, Worth explained innocently that he and Biddle had purchased 400 lbs of cocoa in six bags for personal use in England. Only when they had been told that importation would be difficult had they decided to sell it. But the over-cautious captain smelt a rat. He ordered a check on the frigate's stores, which revealed over 70 bags of cocoa weighing a substantial 5058 lbs which could not be accounted for. Suspecting a large-scale smuggling operation, Vernon had Worth and Biddle arrested and asked for a court martial.[9] To replace them, Hardy appointed his clerk, John Dennis, as Acting Purser, and the Master's Assistant of the *Fly*, George Hingston, to be Acting Master. As a midshipman, Hingston had passed the lieutenant's examination nine years before but had long since given up any hope of promotion and had gone into the cul-de-sac of the navigation branch.

On 2 February 1823 *Creole* returned from Rio de Janeiro and rehoisted Sir Thomas Hardy's broad pennant. She brought news, letters and fresh supplies, but no officer for the *Doris*. A day before the ship had sailed, the chosen man, Lieutenant John Taylor, had resigned his British commission to take up an appointment as captain-of-frigate in the Brazilian Navy. It later emerged that while he had been in the capital, Taylor had had a series of secret meetings with the chief minister during which he had been offered the post. The temptation must clearly have been enormous. Up to that time, Taylor's career had been typical of an officer caught in the slump that followed the Napoleonic Wars. He had served in frigates throughout the conflict, but had been unemployed since the peace and knew that his appointment to *Blossom* was likely to be his last. He may also have found it difficult to make his mark when he had to be described in the *Navy List* as 'John Taylor (c)' to distinguish him from two other lieutenants with the same name. Whatever the reason, he had yielded to temptation and became the only John Taylor in the Brazilian service.

It was highly irregular for a serving officer to resign in these circumstances and Sir Thomas Hardy felt unable to accept Taylor's letter. The Commodore marked him as 'Run' in the ship's books and reported the case to the Admiralty, advising that the matter be treated with moderation in order to avoid problems with the imperial authorities. London, however, took the matter seriously. The efforts being made by the Brazilians to recruit foreign officers and men had raised the spectre of wholesale desertions and, in spite of Hardy's advice, it felt impelled to take a strong line. On 1 April Hardy was ordered to 'avail himself of any occasion that may offer, without violating Brazilian territory or flag, of seeking the deserter and ... bringing him to trial before a court martial'.[10] The lieutenant's vacancy on *Doris* was filled by the promotion of Midshipman George Dyer.

On 11 February the frigate's lengthy wait at Salvador came to an end. With *Creole* now back on watch in Bahia, Hardy was able to order *Doris* northwards as far as Recife to check on the situation in Pernambuco. In the interim, Hardy began to sort out the numerous diplomatic complications the war was causing. On two occasions now, Portuguese warships had removed prominent Brazilians from British vessels – once from the packet *Manchester*. Hardy pondered that one, but decided that no protest was justified as the protection of the British flag did not extend to foreigners.[11] Then a Brazilian decree was issued on 30 December 1822 that authorized privateering against the flag of Portugal.[12] This brought fears of British ships in the South Atlantic being interfered with by indisciplined freebooters. Fortunately it proved to be a false alarm as no privateering commissions were eventually issued. A more serious problem was the consequence of an embargo on all sailings from Rio de Janeiro which had been declared in January to keep secret the departure of a Brazilian flotilla carrying reinforcement for the imperial army in Bahia. Assuming that the embargo did not apply to warships, HMS *Beaver* had put to sea on her way to the Plate and had been promptly fired on by the shore batteries. That caused a diplomatic protest and an exchange of notes which continued for months.[13] Meanwhile the siege dragged on.

CHAPTER 11

BRAZILIAN VICTORY AND
BRITISH NEUTRALITY

Doris returned to Bahia from Pernambuco on 17 March 1823, with news that all was tranquil. She also carried 23 oxen to eke out the squadron's supply of fresh provisions. Ten were sent over immediately to *Creole* and one to the French brig *La Rusé* which, like the two British vessels, was keeping an eye on things in Salvador. Nothing much had happened in Bahia during *Doris*'s absence, but a fortnight later came a dramatic change. On 30 March the Portuguese frigate *Pérola* with a convoy of ten transports carrying 1800 troops from Lisbon dropped anchor in the Bay. This addition to Brigadier Madeira de Melo's strength meant that the sailors manning the defences could now be replaced and the fleet which had lain in semi-idleness for months used for offensive action. Indeed, the *Pérola* carried dispatches ordering Madeira de Melo to put a stop to the Brazilian rebellion once and for all by clamping a blockade on Rio de Janeiro.

The new instructions were at variance with the original orders given to Commodore Félix de Campos and it took a fortnight of argument before a plan was agreed on and ships, stores and munitions were ready. But the Portuguese offensive had come too late. On 19 April the latest addition to the British South America Squadron, HMS *Tartar*, sailed into the bay with dispatches for Sir Thomas Hardy and alarming news of events in Rio. Lord Cochrane with half a dozen British officers had arrived from Chile in the brig *Colonel Allen* to take command of the Imperial Navy. The ships that the Brazilian Government had been so energetically preparing were now ready. Eleven were afloat in Rio de Janeiro harbour – the two-decker *Pedro I*, the frigates *Piranga*, *Niterói* and *Real Carolina*, the corvettes *Maria da Glória* and *Liberal*, the brigs *Guarani* and *Caboclo*, and three brigantines. And, in the nick of time, a first contingent of 170 British officers and men recruited in England had arrived to bring their crews up to minimum strength. Their leader, Captain James Thompson, had been given command of the *Real Carolina*, while *Niterói* had been given to *Blossom*'s erstwhile lieutenant, now Captain John Taylor. The flagship, *Pedro I*, had been entrusted to one of the officers who had come from Chile with Lord Cochrane, a red-headed ex-Royal Navy lieutenant called Thomas Sackville Crosbie. On 29 March the Brazilians had declared Bahia to be under blockade and on 1 April Cochrane had sailed to enforce it.

In Salvador the *Tartar*'s news removed any thought of a Portuguese offensive. Morale nevertheless remained high and there was good reason for the optimism. The Portuguese squadron now consisted of one ship-of-the-line, two frigates, four corvettes, six armed ships and two scouting vessels mounting between them 380 cannon. Against them, the Brazilians had sent six poorly manned ships mounting no more than 234 guns. But even if Madeira de Melo shared the general optimism, he believed in making victory doubly sure when faced with an opponent of Cochrane's reputation. On 22 April, through Vice Consul Follett, he wrote to Sir Thomas Hardy invoking the Anglo-Portuguese defensive alliance, and asking for the help of the British South America Squadron against the Brazilian force. There were at this time four ships of the Royal Navy in Salvador harbour – *Creole*, *Doris*, *Tartar* and another reinforcement from England, the sloop *Fly*. A fifth, the *Beaver*, appeared from Rio de Janeiro the following day while her consorts were firing a 21-gun salute in honour of the birthday of King George. Hardy considered the request but politely declined to intervene, stressing that the treaty only applied to external threats and not to internal disputes. In Brazil, Britain was strictly neutral.[1] Undismayed, the Portuguese prepared for sea. Finally, on 30 April, after a delay when the *Dom João VI* grounded on a sandbank, Commodore de Campos led his force southwards over the horizon to confront Lord Cochrane and the Brazilian Navy.

Amid all the excitement and preparations ashore, the British warships calmly went about their harbour routine, the new vessels transferring fresh provisions to the old, *Doris* supplying all with cocoa from her still extensive stocks. It was 20 months since the frigate had fitted out in the Medway, and her stores, equipment and cordage were beginning to show signs of deterioration. There was now time to survey the most dubious items. Captain Vernon was also concerned that the purser's blue 'slop' trousers were too short to fit men averaging 5 feet 4 inches in height. The trousers were judged to be satisfactory, but the hammocks and quarterdeck awnings were discarded to be replaced from new bolts of canvas. Over 6300 lbs of bread from an early batch were condemned and sent ashore for sale, and the lifts on the lower yards and the tackles and runners securing the masts were replaced. At the same time, the topmasts were refitted and their stays and rigging replaced.[2]

Sir Thomas Hardy also used the opportunity presented by the concentration of so many vessels to reshuffle the officers and survey the sick list resulting from the rigours of the heat and rain of the Brazilian summer. As a result, 20 of the *Doris*'s men were moved or changed. Five sailors, two Royal Marines, the surgeon, the clerk and two lieutenants – Dyer and Lys – were invalided out. Replacements came in the form of Surgeon Binnie, Clerk Hammond and Lieutenant Greene, all from *Tartar*, and the newly promoted Lieutenant Pawlby from *Creole*. A week later, his promotion secured, Pawlby went back to *Creole* in exchange for Lieutenant Thomas Hoste, brother of the victor of the (frigate) Battle of Lissa in 1811. Midshipman Lloyd was also given permission to change ships with Midshipman Leach of the *Fly*. In addition three men were transferred out of *Doris* – the carpenter and the boatswain moving to *Fly* (on his way to a posting on *Blossom)* and First-Class Volunteer C.C. Dawkins to *Creole*, the latter being replaced by Midshipman White. The stays in Bahia and Pernambuco had also provided the opportunity for four desertions, but these, as usual, were replaced by British volunteers from the port.[3]

On 9 May 1823 it was the turn of *Doris* to head for Rio de Janeiro for a change of scenery and to collect supplies for the squadron in Bahia. After an uneventful voyage of seven days the frigate passed the Sugar Loaf and the island of Villegagnon to find *Alacrity* and the frigate *Jupiter* at anchor among the mass of shipping in the harbour. The city was buzzing with rumour and excitement. Brazilian independence had taken a further step forward with the ceremonial opening of the Assembly a fortnight earlier by the Emperor. And the arrival of the *Jupiter*, stopping off on her way to India with the new Governor General of Bengal, Lord Amherst, had also caused enthusiasm. It was rumoured that His Lordship carried secret messages of support from the British Government. But the capital was also in a state of deep anxiety over how Lord Cochrane and the new Brazilian Navy had fared in its challenge to the Portuguese naval squadron in Bahia. *Doris* could tell stories of starvation and shortages in the beleaguered city of Salvador, but had no information about Cochrane's activities.

Alacrity had arrived in Rio shortly before from Valparaiso with 'remittances' from British merchants. She also had two of the *Doris*'s sailors who had 'run' in the Pacific the year before – William Ward and Jonathan Steel. No sooner had the men been restored, however, than two others deserted. Both were notorious bad hats – William Sullivan who, in spite of his starring role as Triton in the Crossing the Line Ceremony, had regularly appeared in *Doris*'s punishment rota, and Jonathan Moore who had been flogged for drunkenness four times since joining from *Superb* only a year earlier. With the *Fly* now heading for Cape Horn to replace her, *Alacrity* was ready to return to England at the end of her tour of duty. Unfortunately she was short of a senior midshipman. Captain Vernon filled the vacancy by transferring William Candler to the brig, then applied himself to the main reason for the visit. In the weeks that followed, every inch of the frigate's hold and decks were filled with provisions. By the 28 May she had loaded 31,000 lbs of bread, 9000 lbs of salt beef and pork, 4700 lbs of flour, 3020 lbs of raisins, 3826 lbs of sugar, 130 bushels of lentils, 23 bullocks, and huge amounts of rope, tallow, tin, copper plate, wood, turpentine and pitch.[4] The volume of supplies being taken on board was so great that the Brazilian Government suspected the British of attempting to break their newly proclaimed blockade of

Bahia and made a diplomatic protest.[5] Sir Thomas Hardy had to issue quick reassurance that the amounts loaded on to *Doris* (and subsequently on to *Creole*) were solely for the use of the British South America Squadron.[6]

Doris reached Cape St Antonio on 4 June. Under a grey sky, fitful squalls and a quartering sea, the frigate sped into the Bay of Bahia, took in sail and came between the forts do Mar and St Philip, joining *Tartar, Beaver* and the latest British reinforcement, the sloop *Brazen*, which had arrived from Spithead ten days before. *Creole* had already sailed for Rio for more supplies, so it was from the main truck of HMS *Tartar* that Sir Thomas Hardy's red, white and blue pennant now flew in the fresh south-easterly breeze. As before there were salutes to be exchanged – 17 guns for the white Portuguese ensign on the fort, 15 for Commodore Felix de Campos's flag on the *Dom João VI*.

But much had happened in Bahia during *Doris*'s absence. On 4 May the Portuguese had met Lord Cochrane's Brazilian squadron and had effectively seen it off. Cochrane had gamely attacked Felix de Campos's tight-knit line of 12 warships, and Captain Thomas Sackville Crosbie had managed to break through in the fast-sailing flagship *Pedro I*, while the frigates *Piranga* and *Niterói*, commanded by the American David Jewitt and the Englishman John Taylor, had engaged from windward. But poor gunnery, shoddy equipment and open obstruction from the disenchanted Portuguese seamen on whom Brazil still depended, had frustrated Cochrane's efforts. And when the Portuguese van had doubled back to face him with overwhelming odds, he had been forced to beat a hasty retreat over the horizon.

Thinking that the Brazilian threat had been neutralized, Commodore de Campos had remained at sea for another two weeks before returning to Salvador. But Lord Cochrane had merely retired to a small base 30 miles to the south to reorganize. There, with typical audacity, he had transferred all his reliable British and Brazilian officers and men to *Pedro I* and the corvette *Maria da Glória* and, in company with the newly arrived frigate *Real Carolina*, had sailed again to enforce the blockade, snapping up the supply vessels on which Salvador was now totally dependent. On 12 June he even attempted a night attack against the Portuguese warships in the port and was only frustrated by a lack of wind.

But for the Brazilian blockade to be legal, it took more than an official declaration. International rules dictated that a blockade was only legitimate if it was continuously maintained by a superior force. The fact that Cochrane had fewer ships than the Portuguese defenders of Bahia therefore caused an immediate technical difficulty. Sir Thomas Hardy pondered the problem and ruled that as far as Britain was concerned, the legal beginning of the blockade was not the time of Cochrane's arrival but the date on which the Portuguese squadron returned permanently to the Bay of Bahia – that is, 2 June 1823. Any ship taken before that date was therefore 'bad' prize and would occasion a vigorous British protest before any prize court. In the middle of June Consul General Chamberlain was asked to inform the Brazilian Government of Hardy's decision in case any British vessels had been arrested before the deadline.[7] Fortunately none had, so no problem arose.

But whatever the legal niceties, in practical terms Cochrane's cutting of Salvador's lifeline by sea reduced the Portuguese to despair – and fury at the inability of Commodore de Campos to do anything about it in spite of his enormous superiority of force. As the weeks passed and supplies dwindled, they resigned themselves to the inevitable. On 20 June the situation was so bad that Military Governor Madeira de Melo ordered the evacuation of the city and of all its public and private property. By 2 July a vast convoy of 17 warships and 75 merchantmen had assembled in the Bay loaded with the contents of the dockyard and the warehouses, packed with troops, and carrying all Portuguese citizens who wished to escape. Meanwhile, outside the Bay, Lord Cochrane waited to pounce with the *Pedro I*, *Real Carolina*, *Niterói*, *Maria da Glória* and the recently arrived brig-of-war *Bahia*. *Bahia* had originally been the *Colonel Allen* which had brought Cochrane from Chile, but in its quest for ships, the Brazilian Government had bought the brig, armed it with cannon and sent it off to reinforce Cochrane with a second instalment of 102 British sailors recently arrived from England. They had also commissioned her captain, Bartholomew Hayden, who had resigned from his post as Second Master on the

Conway two years before to follow his fortune in South America, as a commander in the Brazilian Navy.

As these events unfolded, life for the crews of the watching British warships went on more or less as usual. The only difference was that instead of the normal pattern of general maintenance, a concentrated effort was put on replacing and refurbishing *Doris*'s sails. It took the combined efforts of the squadron's sailmakers two weeks to complete the task. But the stay in Bahia in the heat and humidity of the rainy season was taking its toll on all the ships of the squadron. Fever swelled the sick list, in spite of cleaning and fumigating the lower decks and sprinkling vinegar in the holds. *Tartar*, fresh from England, seemed to suffer most and buried four of her ship's company in a month. Two were young midshipmen. *Doris* did better with only one fatality – the Tahitian seaman Aotaere who had joined the frigate the previous year in Peru. A respectful naval funeral ceremony took place in the Bay the same day. The body was taken from the ship in a pinnace accompanied by the ship's boats, all manned by seamen in white duck and under the command of a uniformed officer. At the chosen spot, the boats grouped together, raised their oars to the vertical as a token of respect and kept them there until the clerk had read the burial service and the deceased had been committed to the deep.[8] The procession then rowed back to the ship with equal solemnity.

Hardy's deployment of his squadron went on apace, the movements of British warships keeping the Imperial Government fully informed of developments in Salvador. On 11 June *Brazen* sailed for Rio de Janeiro on her way to the Plate where she was to keep an eye on events in Montevideo and Buenos Aires.[9] Behind she left a newly promoted Lieutenant Matthias in *Doris* as the replacement for Lieutenant Hoste who had already moved on. She was followed on 14 June by HMS *Bann* of the West Africa Squadron, which had arrived in Salvador in fruitless search of supplies. On 21 June it was the turn of the *Beaver* to carry news to the south.

Tartar and *Doris* remained on watch, loading money and property from British merchants for safekeeping as the day of the evacuation and the Brazilian takeover of Salvador drew near. On 2

July *Creole* was back from her supply run to Rio de Janeiro. Off
Cape St Antonio she met the *Pedro I* and hove to so that Captain
Spencer could climb aboard with letters for Lord Cochrane. Then
she continued into the Bay, its waters filled as far as the eye could
see with the ships of the Portuguese convoy as they filled, backed
and organized themselves. Next day they headed for the open sea.
Lord Cochrane set off in pursuit, his warships shepherding the
convoy out of Brazilian waters while attacking the troopships and
picking up stragglers which the escorts were powerless to protect.
Within days, Cochrane's prizes began to arrive in the harbour of
Salvador. Then, as Hardy and his captains watched, on 4 July 1823
the city was peacefully occupied by the Brazilian army. Next
morning the Bay reverberated to the percussion of saluting guns as
the green and yellow flag of Brazil was raised for the first time
over the forts and the main buildings of the city. The war in Bahia
was over. And it was time for Commodore Hardy to move his
headquarters back to Rio de Janeiro.

On 20 July 1823 His Majesty's Ships *Creole*, *Doris* and *Briton* –
the most recent addition to the South America Squadron – were
back in the Bay of Guanabara to find the imperial capital rejoicing
at the expulsion of the Portuguese and the adhesion of Bahia to
the Brazilian Empire. The news had been brought by the Brazilian
corvette *Liberal* only three days before. There were wild celebra-
tions: the city was illuminated at night, and gala performances were
held in the theatre. The officers of the *Doris* were able to relax
once more amid the friendly bustle of a familiar port. The frigate
began to take on board its regular daily supply of 250 lbs of fresh
beef and 125 lbs of vegetables, supplemented this time by a
welcome 650 oranges. There were sights to see, rides in the
country, and acquaintances to visit. One of them was their old
friend and patroness, Mrs Maria Graham.

Maria had had an adventurous time since they last saw her. In
Valparaiso she had become friends with Lord Cochrane and his
officers, and had been holidaying at his estate at Quinteiro during
the severe earthquakes of November and December 1822. And
when Cochrane, disenchanted with the situation in Chile and Peru,
had accepted the Brazilian offer to command their Navy, she had

travelled round the Horn with him and his officers on the *Colonel Allen*. Now she was back in Rio de Janeiro, living in a small house on the Gloria Hill close to her friends, the Mays. Unable to return to England by a recurrence of her consumption, Mrs Graham was making the most of her time in Brazil and preparing yet another book for publication. With an intellectual curiosity that more than compensated for her poor physical health, she was investigating every aspect of life, visiting the commercial quarter, the warehouses, the arsenal, the dockyard, the foundling hospital, the botanical gardens, the library, the theatre, the forts and the churches, as well as the great estates, Indian settlements and farms of the interior. Inevitably she had taken advantage of the opportunity to study slavery at first hand, finding the practice repugnant. She went to the slave market and the plantations. She calculated the size of the Brazilian slave trade, finding that, in 1822, 24,934 souls had been imported through Rio de Janeiro alone. She proved to her own satisfaction that slavery was not only immoral and degrading to all involved but was also profoundly uneconomic.[10]

On the lighter side, Maria Graham was also establishing a modest place in the Rio social scene, and mixing with the local aristocracy as well as the British community. She made friends with the Baronessa de Campos, with her daughter, who was the wife of the new foreign minister, and with the family of the Viscondessa do Rio Seco, although as a widow of modest means she found it difficult to keep up with their wealth and lifestyle. At times she was deeply lonely and welcomed the chance to see her old friends from *Doris*, especially 'her boys' – the younger midshipmen on whom she had lavished so much attention. They took rides together in the evening and enjoyed the lush greenery in the hills around the city. On one occasion they went through the fortifications to see the Praia Vermelha, an idyllic sandy cove between the foot of the Sugar Loaf and the broad sweep of Copacabana, and lingered so long that that they were locked in and had to wait until the guard was turned out and sent to find the key.

But there were now few familiar faces on the *Doris*. It was two years since the frigate had left Sheerness under Captain Graham's command, and there had been numerous changes in her complement. Of the five original commissioned officers, only the capable and gentlemanly Lieutenant William Dance remained. And of 16 midshipmen and volunteers, only six – Matthew Forster, Charles Blatchley, James Turner, Jonathan Montgomery, Charles Bosanquet and William Maude – were left. The same was true of the 11 senior and 'inferior' warrant officers. All had gone but Gunner Nesbitt, Schoolmaster Hyslop and Acting Surgeon Kift. Likewise, of the 213 seamen, petty officers, boys and Royal Marines who had been aboard when *Doris* had left Plymouth, only 134 were still there.[11]

And there were more changes in the offing. Sir Thomas Hardy had received news of events in the Pacific and the River Plate which he felt should be sent urgently to London. In Peru a royalist army was on the verge of retaking Lima, Bolivar was rushing troops to reinforce the patriot government, and the Peruvian Navy under Admiral Guise had declared a blockade of the coast. In Chile a new government under General Freyre had taken peaceful control. And in Buenos Aires the continual civil disputes in the city seemed likely to be calmed by what appeared to be an imminent peace treaty with Spain that would at last recognize the independence of the United Provinces of the River Plate. As soon as HMS *Eclaire* arrived from England to replace her, *Beaver* was due to return home. Hardy decided to accelerate her sailing date so that she could carry the news.[12] Her departure would also enable him to solve another knotty problem.

Purser Worth and Master Biddle had been for six months under open arrest on *Doris* facing changes of smuggling. Their presence was a continual source of embarrassment, and attempts to get them invalided out on health grounds had failed. It had also proved impossible to assemble the number of captains needed for a court martial locally, so Hardy determined to send both men back to England for trial. He decided that they should go on *Beaver*, together with those who would be needed to give evidence. On 6 August the brig sailed for Portsmouth carrying Hardy's dispatches, the two accused and the principal witnesses – Captain Vernon, Lieutenant Dance, Volunteers Maude and Dawkins, and a couple of petty officers. Also on board the *Beaver* were *Doris*'s invalids, the unfortunate Lieutenant MacDonald who had been left behind by *Conway*, and the second Tahitian seaman, Arape, who was being brought back to England on compassionate grounds. He was eventually discharged to the London Missionary Society to be sent home.[13] To lessen the impact of these moves on his already overstretched supply of senior officers, Hardy decided to give William Dance command of *Beaver* on promotion, and to move Thomas Bourchier, the brig's current commander, to *Doris* as Acting Captain.[14] Bourchier had left Spithead four years earlier as Hardy's flag lieutenant. His move to *Doris* was his second significant promotion in less than two years. Another beneficiary was Admiralty Midshipman Charles Blatchley, promoted lieutenant to replace Dance.

CHAPTER 12

PROMOTION AND 'INTEREST' IN THE SOUTH AMERICA SQUADRON

Charles Drinkwater was a skilled and talented young officer. He joined the Royal Navy in 1816 at the age of 13, and had seen service in the *Northumberland*, taking Napoleon to exile in St Helena, and the *Leander*, before he was appointed as midshipman in Sir Thomas Hardy's flagship *Superb* to go to the South America station in 1819. He went on to pass the lieutenant's examination with flying colours in the Peruvian port of Callao on 24 January 1822 before Captains White of *Superb*, Vernon of *Blossom* and Hall of *Conway*. Indeed, his performance in navigation and astronomy was so striking that Basil Hall actually mentioned it in a book describing his South American experiences which was published two years later.[1] Charles Drinkwater's personal qualities were also admirable, so much so that a family friend reported to his father in November 1820 that the flagship's first lieutenant had said to him 'We have 50 mids on this ship sir, and Drinkwater is the finest young man amongst them.'[2]

But in addition to being both competent and personable, Charles had that most necessary of early nineteenth-century professional assets – the right family and the right connections. His father, the notable Colonel John Drinkwater, had been a spectator at the Battle of St Vincent in 1797, and it was his effusive book *A Narrative of the Proceedings of the British Fleet. By an Officer of HM Land Forces*, with its descriptions and reportage of Nelson's conversations and heroism, that had done so much to establish the latter's public reputation. He had subsequently obtained the job of comptroller in charge of army accounts. Colonel Drinkwater was thus a confidant of Nelson, a friend of his son's commander-in-chief, Sir Thomas Hardy, and a close government contact of Sir George Cockburn of the Admiralty Board. With connections and 'interest' like this, his son's rapid promotion to lieutenant should have been assured. Yet it was not so. It was made plain to Charles from the beginning that he had to join a queue, and it took four years before he managed to get an appointment as lieutenant.

There were of course rules that governed the first vital step from the humble rank of midshipman to the commissioned glory of lieutenant. Candidates had to be at least 19 years old, have had six years' sea experience and had to pass a rigorous oral examination. But in the Royal Navy, people were not just appointed in general terms to the rank of lieutenant: they had to be appointed as lieutenant of a named ship. In the period after 1815 the number of vessels at sea was minute in comparison with the heydays of the Napoleonic Wars, and with 85 per cent of existing officers without employment, it became enormously difficult to find a ship into which a qualified midshipman could be appointed as lieutenant. Indeed, one of the phenomena of the time was the elderly 'passed midshipman' – an officer who had fulfilled all the requirements, but was still waiting in his old rank for a lieutenant's vacancy which, as often as not, never came.

And this of course is where 'interest', pull and connections came in. Interest was all-pervasive even in late Georgian times, and it is easy to jump to the conclusion that with seagoing berths so scarce, naval appointments and promotion would be dominated by string-pulling and that lordlings and the relations of politicians would be given priority over the heads of officers who were more experienced and deserving. But if the experience of the South America Squadron is anything to go by, this description is very far from the truth.

There seem to have been two major reasons for this. First, the Navy was a highly professional force, and demanded technical competence from everyone, whatever their connections. Secondly, a new form of interest appeared on the scene in the post-war

1. HMS *Doris* at sea. W.F. Mitchell. National Maritime Museum.

2. *Doris* fitting out for South America. Attributed to T.L. Hornbrook. National Maritime Museum.

3. A frigate off Barn Point, Plymouth. T.L. Hornbrook. National Maritime Museum.

4a. (left) Sir Thomas Hardy, Commander-in-Chief of the South American station, 1819–1823. Pelligrini. National Maritime Museum.

4b. (right) Rear Admiral Sir Robert Otway, who ordered *Doris'* abandonment in 1829. National Maritime Museum.

5. Rio de Janeiro showing units of the South America squadron. Martinet, Heaton and Rensberg. National Maritime Museum.

6. *Doris* going round Cape Horn. T.L. Hornbrook (?) National Maritime Museum.

7. The port of Valparaiso. J. S... ...ional Maritime Museum.

8. *Doris* being surveyed in Valparaiso before condemnation, October 1828. T.L. Hornbrook (?) National Maritime Museum.

period which favoured the humble and the experienced. This was rooted in the sheer loyalty felt by both the Admiralty and individual commanders to those who had fought with them during the late wars, and a desire to see that deserving junior officers, whatever their social origins, could look forward to some sort of financial security during the cold days of the post-war slump. It was the same altruism that had caused the Admiralty to promote 995 midshipmen to the rank of lieutenant at the end of the war in 1815. As a commissioned officer, of course, an individual received half pay when unemployed; as a midshipman he received nothing. Another result was the introduction of the Admiralty Midshipman scheme in 1818, explicitly designed to ensure that deserving veterans not only got naval appointments but received Admiralty backing and priority in the struggle for promotion to lieutenant.

There was clearly enormous competition for both appointments and promotion, and, like *Doris*, all ships in the South America Squadron carried complements of midshipmen well above their establishments. Sir Thomas Hardy's flagship *Superb*, for example, had no fewer than 38 on board (13 of whom were Admiralty Midshipmen) in place of the 18 that a 74-gun ship usually carried.[3] All were eager, if not desperate, for promotion and, indeed, 29 of them were lucky and eventually made it to lieutenant, although only 18 managed it before Hardy's period of command finished at the end of 1823.

Acts of outstanding heroism apart, to get a chance of promotion a midshipman's name had to appear on one of two lists. The first was the Admiralty's, the second belonged to the local commander-in-chief. The two lists were supposed to be confidential, but Charles Drinkwater's letters show that they were a source of continuing speculation and gossip. By the time Hardy reached the South Atlantic in 1819, it had become established that lieutenant vacancies resulting from death or court martial were filled from the commander-in-chief's list, while vacancies caused by sickness or desertion were filled from the Admiralty's.[4] Since many more came as a result of officers being invalided out than all other causes put together, this naturally gave the Admiralty men the best chance. As Hardy ruefully explained in a personal letter in July

1820, he had been 'unable to promote Mr Cox as no-one will die'![5] In fact there were fewer than half a dozen promotions due to fatalities during his four-year tenure of command.

It is also clear that to protect senior officers from undue outside pressure as much as to restrain personal whim, special promotion procedures were introduced. When Sir Robert Peel – a powerful political ally of Sir George Cockburn – approached the Admiral in support of a candidate for promotion in 1826, he was obliged to ask not for direct intervention but for guidance on the procedure that had to be followed. Even Lord Wellesley was given a procedural excuse for difficulties in securing promotion for one of his nominees, a Mr Greene.[6] Likewise, Charles Drinkwater's promotion eventually came as a result of his following a procedural suggestion made by Cockburn in response to pressure applied by his father. It consisted of his returning to England, taking the lieutenant's examination again at the Royal Naval College Portsmouth and then getting a place on the Admiralty List reserved for 'collegians'. Charles followed this advice and was duly promoted. The Admiralty acted as another safeguard. Hardy, for example, was under pressure from friends in Dorset to get a certain Midshipman Daniel Cox promoted. He was able to appoint him temporarily as flag lieutenant as an act of generosity when the young man's father went bankrupt, but the Admiralty were lukewarm and only agreed to confirm his promotion as a gesture when Hardy returned after his period of command.[7] Cox was never employed again.

To get on to these promotion lists certainly required interest, but it came in different types and degrees. The most obvious was to have the good fortune of being related to a nobleman or person of political influence. Another was to have naval connections in terms of being related to a flag officer or a senior Admiralty official. There were men with both types of pull in Sir Thomas Hardy's command. But the most striking feature of the promotion system was the predominance of a third form of interest by which both the Admiralty and the commander-in-chief chose to give preference to veterans. Indeed, the great majority of men who were promoted as far as lieutenant in the South America Squadron seemed to owe their good fortune to their service records and not to other considerations. Thus, if being designated as an Admiralty Midshipman is defined as possessing 'interest', then in the post-war period the majority of junior naval officers had it in one form or another. Indeed, there seemed to be more interest around than there were jobs. No wonder Charles Drinkwater, with all his influential connections, had to wait.

The promotions that took place in the South America Squadron during the second half of Hardy's tenure as commander-in-chief – that is, from October 1821 to October 1823 – illustrate this. During this period there were 15 ships on station. Five – the frigates *Aurora*, *Doris* and *Creole*, the sloop *Blossom* and the brig *Alacrity* – were there for the whole time. The others were present for only part of it. The 74-gun *Superb*, the frigate *Owen Glendower*, the sloops *Conway* and *Slaney* and the brig *Beaver* returned to England in the middle of this two-year period, being replaced by the frigates *Brazen*, *Tartar* and *Briton*, and the sloops *Eclaire* and *Fly*. There were therefore 45 lieutenants present in 15 ships on the South America station between 1821 and 1823, although the number was happily increased to 47 when the Admiralty decreed in mid-1822 that 10-gun brigs like *Alacrity* and *Beaver* should carry an extra officer.[8]

Turnover at the level of lieutenant was rapid, and during this two-year period, no fewer than 26 midshipmen were promoted either from the Admiralty List or from Hardy's own. Of the 24 young men whose backgrounds are known, 19 had fought in the Napoleonic Wars, of whom only four (two on the Admiralty List, two on Hardy's) had the additional advantage of naval or political connections. The ages and ratings as Admiralty Midshipmen of the two promotees for whom there is no background information suggest that they too were war veterans, bringing the total in this group to 21.[9] None of the remaining five young men had pre-1815 service, but all had powerful family or naval interest. They were the Hon. E. Wodehouse, son of a lord and nephew of an admiral; Lord William Paget, son of the Marquis of Anglesey who had commanded the cavalry at Waterloo; G.T. Purvis, son of a secretary to Lords Howe and St Vincent and cousin to Captain J.B.

Purvis; George Dyer, son of the Admiralty's Chief Clerk; and Charles Drinkwater himself.

The striking thing about the Admiralty nominees is that the great majority (15, probably 17 out of 21) had clearly been selected in recognition of their war and service records. Six had also served at the bombardment of Algiers in 1816. Two had political or naval interest as well, being Francis Grove, son of a Lord Lieutenant of Stafford and nephew of Lord Cartsfort, and Alexander Bridport Becher, godson of the admiral whose name he carried and son of Captain Alexander Becher RN. Becher, serving on *Conway*, was also establishing a reputation for himself as a hydrographer.

The same pattern is seen in the commander-in-chief's list, though probably for another reason. Hardy was a Dorset man who had no aristocratic relations to appease. As a result, four of his nominees were 'followers', that is – as he explained in one of his letters to Colonel Drinkwater – 'young men who served with me in the American War' between 1812 and 1815.[10] Only two of these were well connected – the Hon. Thomas Best, son of a chief justice and brother-in-law of an admiral, and Patrick Blake, nephew of a Captain RN, son of an Irish baronet and grandson of Sir Thomas Gage, the American War of Independence commander. Those who were not 'followers' in this sense were either Dorset men or relations of Hardy's naval acquaintances. The first group did badly in the race for lieutenant, but the second did better. It included George Dyer; Charles Hallowell, son of Sir Benjamin Hallowell who had commanded the *Swiftsure* at the Battle of the Nile and was now commander-in-chief at the Nore; Horatio Nelson Atkinson, son of the sailing master of the *Victory* at Trafalgar who was now master attendant at Portsmouth Dockyard; and Horatio Thomas Austin, a 'follower' with a Nelson connection since his father had been wounded at the Nile as boatswain of the *Vanguard.* Inevitably, young Hallowell was a lieutenant by 1820, while Atkinson had to wait six more years, was never re-employed and, like many officers in his position, ended up in the coastguard. Austin, on the other hand, rose by sheer ability to the top of the tree.

The majority of new lieutenants may have been chosen from

the ranks of the worthy and the experienced, but at the higher level of commander and captain it was a different story. All of the seven men promoted to this level during the last two years of Sir Thomas Hardy's command did have powerful interest. The four who became commanders were Thomas Porter, son of a bishop; William Dance of the *Doris*, a 'follower' of Hardy who had served on the North America station; William Fanshawe Martin, son of Vice Admiral Sir Thomas Byam Martin, Comptroller of the Navy; and Thomas Bourchier, Hardy's flag lieutenant, son of a major general, and Admiral Sir Edward Codrington's future son-in-law. It was this Bourchier who was appointed Acting Captain of *Doris* in Vernon's absence. Likewise, the three commanders who became full captains were heavyweights in terms of interest. They were Archibald Maclean, son of a Scottish laird and grandson of the Earl of Hopetown; the Hon. Frederick Spencer, son of Earl Spencer, a former First Lord; and William James Hope Johnstone, son of the current first naval lord at the Admiralty. At this level, interest more than compensated for youth. Spencer and Hope Johnstone were only in their mid-20s, and Martin was just 22 years old. Thereafter nicknamed 'Fly Martin' after the sloop into which he was promoted, the youthful captain immediately instituted a series of remorseless drills and punishments which turned the crew into automata and drove his first lieutenant to despair and a nervous breakdown. Martin and Hope Johnstone both ended their careers as admirals.

The majority of vacancies at the level of lieutenant (14 out of 26) on the South America station were inevitably the result of illness. But promotion prospects were improved at the end of 1821 when the *Conway* unexpectedly lost two lieutenants – Horatio Darby, who deserted in Callao guilt-ridden at the detection of his rampant homosexuality, and Charles Legge, who sadly died in Valparaiso. A year later, two events caused a greater stir in the squadron. The first was the death of Captain Thomas Graham of the *Doris*, a circumstance which was deeply regretted but which nevertheless caused excitement since it unlocked no fewer than three promotions – commander to captain, lieutenant to commander, and midshipman to lieutenant. Commander Maclean, Flag

Lieutenant Bourchier and Admiralty Midshipman Liddell of the *Aurora* were the lucky ones. Since this vacancy was caused by a death, it should properly have been filled from the list of the commander-in-chief, but as Hardy had earlier put one of his men into a gap which should have been filled by the Admiralty, he was forced to promote Liddell by way of compensation.[11]

The second stir was caused by the resignation of Lieutenant John Taylor of the *Blossom* to join the Brazilian Navy. Resignations by petty officers of His Majesty's ships were not rare – indeed *Conway* had lost two men in this way – Midshipman William Eyre and Second Master Bartholomew Hayden. John Taylor's subsequent performance in the Brazilian War of Independence was so spectacular that it made him a national hero, but the Admiralty was indignant that a commissioned officer should take such a step, refused to accept Taylor's resignation and marked him as a deserter in the ship's books. Midshipman Dyer was promoted to fill the vacancy. For the next ten years, the British Government conducted a minor campaign aimed at getting Taylor dismissed from the Imperial Navy, and it was only in 1832 that it relented. In Brazil Taylor went from strength to strength and eventually retired a vice admiral.[12] Coincidentally, Eyre and Hayden also joined the Brazilian service, fought throughout the independence campaigns, the war against Buenos Aires and in the rebellions of the 1830s. Both eventually reached the rank of commodore.[13]

Whatever the level, the system seemed clear to those who were runners in the promotion race, but occasionally it needed to be massaged. In March 1822 the veteran Captain Thomas White of *Creole* was pushing 60 and known to be willing to quit the fatigues of the South America station. The officers who topped respectively the Admiralty Lists for promotion to captain and commander – the Hon. Frederick Spencer and Thomas Porter – both of whom, according to Drinkwater 'want promotion very bad', had a solution. In Charles's ('Very Secret') words, 'they together made up £5000, which of course has made Captain White very ill and so he is going home.'[14] White was invalided out to a well-funded retirement, Spencer moved into his post in *Creole*, and Porter took the Hon. Frederick's place in command of *Alacrity*. Everyone got what they wanted – even Midshipman Horatio Austin became a lieutenant. It did not take Porter long to recoup his investment. When *Alacrity* was ordered home in mid-1823 she carried a 'freight' of coin and bullion deposited by local British merchants worth £200,000.[15] Commander Porter would have received £2000 as his percentage for the service. Similar massaging happened a year later. Mr Midshipman Drinkwater knew in 1823 when he returned to Brazil in *Briton* having passed the lieutenant's examination a second time, that he was top of the Admiralty List and that the next vacancy would be his. He had also heard that Lieutenant Frampton of the *Doris* (ex-Admiralty Midshipman and veteran of Algiers, promoted the previous year) was ill but refused to be invalided out because he could not find the £80 fare home by packet from Rio. They came to an understanding. Drinkwater discreetly paid half the cost of the ticket via his prize agent. The ailing Frampton was invalided out, and on 9 August Charles Drinkwater at last got his promotion to HMS *Doris*.[16] It was to be the first step in a career in which he would rise to the rank of admiral – one of the three members of the frigate's company who would do so.

CHAPTER 13

CHANGES IN COMMAND

The arrival of Sir Thomas Hardy and his officers gave a fillip to the Rio de Janeiro social scene. There were dances, parties and picnics. Establishing his headquarters in a villa in the Bay of Botafogo between the city and the Sugar Loaf, the Commodore threw a series of highly successful balls with supper for prominent Brazilians and leading members of the British and French communities. Hardy was big in both stature and personality, a proven leader and a tactful diplomat. He had an avuncular good nature and was, in Maria Graham's words, 'not only cheerful and sociable himself but the cause of cheerfulness in others'.[1]

But it was not all partying. A problem that had to be addressed was the alarming level of desertion by sailors from British merchant ships in order to join the Brazilian Navy. There were tempting bounties and Lord Cochrane's reputation was a magnet for the adventurous. Indeed, writing to the junta of Pernambuco in a published letter on 11 July, Cochrane had not only asked for the recruitment of men, but had specified that he wanted British sailors above all others. Consul General Chamberlain and Hardy put in a successful joint protest in September, which resulted in an order banning officers of the Imperial Navy – one third of whom were British themselves at this time – from accepting foreign seamen unless they had certificates from their consuls showing they were free from any other engagement.[2] Nevertheless, to be on the safe side, Hardy instructed his own captains to be extra vigilant and to make sure that boats' crews were prevented from setting foot on shore.[3]

Hardy was also thinking of England. His three-year period of command had already been extended by 12 months, and he now expected news of the arrival of his successor, Rear Admiral Sir George Eyre. Meanwhile, with the struggle for Bahia now settled in favour of Brazil, it was time to redeploy the South America Squadron in the face of unrest breaking out in other parts of the continent. In June Captain Willes of HMS *Brazen* had been sent to keep an eye on the volatile situation developing in the River Plate.[4] On 11 August, only a week since her new Captain Bourchier had taken command, *Doris* was ordered on a cruise to north-eastern Brazil to relieve the *Tartar* in Bahia, then to check on Pernambuco and Paraíba.[5] Captain Brown in *Tartar* was to head for the Pacific where he was to act as senior officer taking *Aurora* and *Fly* under his command.[6] And on 5 September the *Eclaire*, newly arrived from England, was sent north to Maranhão and Pará to safeguard British property in response to rumours of fighting between Brazilian patriots and the Portuguese who were still in occupation.[7] Two weeks after that, Hardy himself sailed south in *Creole* to pour oil on the troubled waters of the River Plate where Captain Willes had immediately managed to antagonize the Government of Buenos Aires.[8] Sir Murray Maxwell, in *Briton*, was left to watch Rio de Janeiro.

When Lieutenant Charles Drinkwater climbed aboard *Doris* on 5 August, the impact of the changes in personnel during the frigate's two-year tour of duty were plain to see. Of the five commissioned sea officers, only Lieutenant Greene had a substantive appointment. All the others, from the captain downwards, were 'acting' pending Admiralty approval. Likewise, of the six warrant officers (the post of chaplain was vacant) only Gunner Nesbitt and Carpenter Moffat had permanent appointments. All the others – master, purser, surgeon, and boatswain – were 'acting'. And whereas there had been 16 midshipmen, master's mates and first-class volunteers crowded into the frigate's gunroom when she left Plymouth, now there were only ten (and two of these – Fowke and Anson – would shortly be posted). This did not mean, however, that *Doris* was being commanded and run by men without experience. Captain Bourchier was 32 years old, and had been at sea since he had entered HMS *Princess Royal* in 1800 and had served in the Channel, the West Indies, the North Sea and

North America. Lieutenants Matthias and Blatchley were veterans as well, having enrolled as first-class volunteers in *Courageous* and *Royal William* respectively in 1809–10 and having seen service in the Channel, the Baltic and the East Indies before being appointed Admiralty Midshipmen on *Brazen* and *Doris*. Lieutenant Greene was the same age but less experienced, having begun his career in *Tonnant* in 1812, and serving in the West Indies and the Channel before being posted as an Admiralty Midshipman in *Beaver*.[9]

Doris's cruise to the north-east lasted ten weeks, half of the time spent safely in the harbour of Salvador. Fortunately the weather was agreeable. Only off Cape Frio on the outward journey did it deteriorate with sudden squalls and heavy rain which drummed on the frigate's decks as she thrashed ahead amid black clouds and distant lightning. For the rest of the time, there were fresh winds from the east with *Doris* sailing easily over a blue sea under topsails, topgallants and even royals and a flying jib.[10] Politically there was nothing for the frigate to report. Pernambuco, Paraíba and Bahia were tranquil, if uneasy, with the imperial authorities apparently well in control. For Charles Drinkwater there was a minor personal disappointment. As a show of gratitude for her husband's interest in his son's promotion, Colonel Drinkwater had suggested that he present Lady Melville with a bouquet of artificial flowers made at the Convent of Solidad in Bahia. The skill of the nuns in making these articles from the feathers of the brilliantly coloured local birds was famous. Unfortunately, on arrival Charles found that the siege of the city had disrupted the supply of feathers and that production had temporarily ceased. Colonel Drinkwater would have to present Lady Melville with a more mundane token of appreciation.

Whether in harbour or at sea, the frigate's man-of-war routine went on. There was the usual maintenance of sails and rigging, divine service and the Articles of War on Sunday, the washing of clothes twice weekly, and the cleaning of the lower decks every fortnight. In her last weeks in Bahia, *Doris* also underwent a thorough facelift. The exterior of the frigate was scraped and repainted in pristine white and black, the standing rigging was re-tarred, and the running rigging reset and repaired. All the boats were then overhauled and repainted. The basics were the same, but Thomas Bourchier's style was clearly different to that of Captain Vernon. Exercises by the Royal Marines and small arms men were reduced to two days a month, and the weekly practices by divisions of the guns which had been a feature of Vernon's time were replaced by a drill at general quarters every two months. Just as notable was the relaxation in discipline. In the seven months of Captain Bourchier's command, there were only ten floggings totalling 276 lashes — mostly for repeated neglect of duty or drunkenness. Although the punishments were infrequent — four took place on the same day — they gave him an 'average' of 1½ floggings and 40 lashes a month — less than half of Captain Vernon's record.[11] And from this time on, desertion ceased to be a reason for a flogging but was defined as 'straggling' — or absence without leave — and was treated as such. Instead of going to the gratings, the 13 deserters who jumped ship and were recovered during this period were punished by having £3 deducted from their pay.

Bourchier also seemed to pay more attention to the crew's well being. Issues of slop clothing were more frequent, and there was greater emphasis on 'making and mending' the crew's garments. And to increase the success rate of the men's attempts at fishing in Bahia, the foreyard was lowered to deck level to provide a better platform for the ship's anglers. There were three desertions this time, all able seamen — John Foster and two incorrigibles, William Ward and Robert Campbell. One of the original members of the crew, Ward had jumped ship in Valparaiso the year before and had been returned by *Alacrity* in May. Now, four months later, he leaped overboard and swam for it. Robert Campbell had deserted in Bahia in November 1821 and had had six months of liberty before being apprehended. Now he was off again. However, the vacancies were filled by three local volunteers and the return of two other deserters, William Sullivan and Andrew Stewart, who were handed over by *Eclaire* on her voyage to the north.

After a three-week stay in Salvador, it was time to go. On 13 October *Doris* weighed anchor and stood out of the Bay bound for the Brazilian capital. She had a comfortable cruise, with light breezes and occasional rain until, ten days later, she passed between the Sugar Loaf and the Fort of Santa Cruz to rejoin *Briton* in the harbour of Rio de Janeiro. Unknowingly she had passed at sea, only the day before, an old friend on her outward voyage to England. For, after an exciting and exhausting stay of six months in the capital which was to result in her *Journal of a Voyage to Brazil and Residence There* ... with its colourful and intimate account of life, manners, food and social habits in the new empire, Maria Graham's health had sufficiently recovered for her to face the Atlantic crossing. But she would be back. During her stay she had been a frequent visitor to the Court and had established a close relationship with the Empress Leopoldina. Now, as the result of a happy suggestion by Sir Thomas Hardy, she had been invited to return to become governess to the little Princess Maria da Glória. As Maria Graham boarded the packet *Chichester* for the passage home loaded with newspapers and happy anticipation, her only regret was that she would not be present to see Lord Cochrane's triumphant return to Rio de Janeiro at the conclusion of the war at sea.[12]

For much had happened while *Doris* had been away. On the negative side, there had been a political crisis that had led to the dismissal of the patriarch of Brazilian independence, José Bonifácio de Andrada e Silva, and the emergence in the Constituent Assembly of radical forces that – to the Emperor's annoyance – were increasingly anti-monarchical. But on the positive side, the country's independence was now assured. For months the capital had thrilled to the news of Cochrane's exploits and marvelled as his prizes began to fill the harbour. There were now over 65 captured vessels riding at their anchors worth £200,000. Cochrane's achievement had been formidable. First, he had completed the blockade that had driven the Portuguese from Bahia. Then he had secured the union of the key northern province of Maranhão to the Empire by means of an audacious ruse. Appearing alone off the provincial capital in the *Pedro I*, he had threatened invasion by a vast and imaginary Brazilian fleet and army, which he claimed was over the horizon, and had tricked the Portuguese garrison into evacuation. And only two days after *Doris*'s arrival, news arrived that one of Cochrane's officers, Commander John

Pascoe Grenfell of the Brazilian Navy, had played the same trick on the Portuguese in Pará and that the huge province of Amazonas too was now part of the Empire. Only in Montevideo were the Portuguese holding out, and that clearly would not last long. Then, on 9 November 1823, Lord Cochrane returned to the Brazilian capital to a hero's welcome. To general rejoicing, he and his officers were loaded with medals and titles. There were parades, gala performances at the theatre, and the city was illuminated for nights on end in celebration.

In their modest way the British were also due for a touch of ceremonial. On 17 November, on a cloudy morning amid light rain, the 74-gun *Spartiate* appeared heading past the Sugar Loaf carrying a new commander-in-chief for the South America Squadron, Rear Admiral Sir George Eyre. The harbour was already thick with warships. There was *Doris*, *Mersey* – the latest addition to the squadron from England – *Creole* which had returned from the Plate the week before, two French frigates, three big Brazilian men-of-war and a Russian frigate. Once again the Bay reverberated to the thunder of gun salutes. There were 21 guns for the green and yellow imperial flag on the forts, 13 for Sir Thomas Hardy's broad pennant, 17 for the French Rear Admiral Grivel in *Astrée*, 19 for Lord Cochrane in the *Pedro I*, and 11 for Consul General Chamberlain who had hastened aboard the new British flagship.[13] The transfer was immediate and, to another 13-gun salute, Eyre's flag was hoisted to the mizzenmast of *Spartiate* the following day to signify the change in command. *Doris* and the other ships in the squadron immediately changed their red ensigns to white to signify that they were now under the command of a rear admiral of the White.

Creole prepared for sea, provisioning for the homeward voyage and receiving the squadron's sick. *Doris* transferred 13 invalids, including Lieutenant Wylde of the Royal Marines. To make up the frigate's numbers, *Spartiate* transferred eight men from her crew, all convicted smugglers serving a five-year term in the Navy as an alternative to imprisonment. The deserter Robert Campbell was also out of luck. After only a few weeks' freedom in Bahia he had been apprehended and was now returned aboard *Briton*. Meanwhile there was a busy coming and going of ships' boats as the squadron's officers were rowed over to *Creole* to say goodbye to old friends and pay their respects to their popular former commander. Then on 25 November the frigate was towed into the fairway while the crews of *Doris* and the other British warships in the harbour manned the yards and gave three cheers as the Rear Admiral and the Commodore were rowed past in Eyre's barge.[14] The following day *Creole* made sail, dipped her ensign to the forts guarding the entrance and disappeared over the horizon bound for England.

CHAPTER 14

PLAYACTING AND BLOCKADE

The new British commander-in-chief lacked Sir Thomas Hardy's bulk, outsize personality and his spectacular war record. He was, however, a veteran of some distinction, having been promoted to captain of the sloop *Prompt* as early as 1796, and serving thereafter in the West Indies, the Eastern Mediterranean and off the coast of Spain. As captain of the *Magnificent* and senior naval officer, he had been instrumental in the capture of a series of enemy convoys and strategic islands in the Adriatic and had received a knighthood for his efforts. Charles Drinkwater found him a charming man – and a useful one, for Eyre's son, William, was an ensign in the army (he was to end up as a major general) and had travelled with his father to Rio de Janeiro en route to joining his regiment at the Cape of Good Hope. With him, he carried letters of introduction to his military superiors provided by Charles's father, Colonel John Drinkwater.

The work carried out in Bahia had left the *Doris* in good condition, and only routine maintenance and cleaning were needed during her stay in Rio de Janeiro, although with temperature and humidity rising as the Brazilian summer advanced, special measures had to be taken once more to air the lower decks and rig awnings to provide shelter from the sun and the occasional tropical storm. Captain Bourchier also took the opportunity to clear, clean and whitewash the spirit and bread rooms, and to have the frigate's equipment and cordage surveyed. The result was that pounds of bread, a 17-inch anchor cable and the breeching ropes and tackles of the guns were condemned and replaced. But for the ship's officers there was plenty of time for leisure, trips ashore and picnics. On one bathing excursion, Drinkwater dropped his watch over the side of the boat and thought he had seen the last of it. Fortunately it stuck on a ledge of rock and was retrieved by one of *Briton*'s midshipmen.

Early in December the younger officers of the four British warships in the harbour decided on a project to pass the time. The idea was to present a performance of Goldsmith's play *She Stoops to Conquer* (twinned with a short comedy about servants called *High Life Below Stairs*) in the Rio Opera House, the ticket money to be donated to the Hospital da Misericordia. There were plenty of volunteers, rehearsals went on apace and in only two weeks it was ready. Only the costumes were delayed, being delivered so late on the evening of the performance that the Emperor Pedro, who had graced the event with his presence, was heard to demand loudly when the show would begin.

In spite of this hiccup, and the fact that it was the height of summer with the thermometer standing at over 80°F in the candlelit theatre, the play took place before an audience of 1000 persons on 19 December 1823. The performance was complemented by fiddlers and music and by a brief appearance by the corps de ballet. The officers of the *Doris* were prominent in the production and provided no fewer than eight members of the cast. The part of Diggory was played by Lieutenant Markham (newly arrived to replace Charles Blatchley, now moved to *Briton*), while those of Marlow, Young Marlow, Roger, and Miss Neville were performed by Midshipmen Noble, Anson, Montgomery and Bosanquet. Stingo was portrayed by Acting Master George Hingston and Mat Muggins by the new clerk, William Hammond. Charles Drinkwater came into his own as Mrs Hardcastle, dressed in a dazzling semi-transparent dress over a yellow slip and with a red scarf, white gloves, yellow shoes and a grotesque wig two feet tall and trimmed with blue ribbons. In spite of more delays owing to repeated demands for the national anthem, cheers for the Emperor and occasional puzzlement arising from the language problem, the play was received with the same enthusiasm with which it was performed, by – to quote Drinkwater – 'a Royal,

14 Playbill for the Squadron's Production
National Maritime Museum London

crowded and delighted audience'.[1]

But *Doris*'s amateur actors did not have long to enjoy their triumph. In November the Emperor had grown tired of the antics of the Constituent Assembly, had suspended its sessions and had surrounded it with troops and artillery to ensure obedience. The delegates had brazened it out for 24 tense and exhausting hours, but eventually submitted. As they filed wearily out, José Bonifácio's brother, Antonio Carlos, had expressed the feelings of them all when he had bowed and said 'I obey the sovereign of the world, His Majesty the Cannon'. The brothers were immediately exiled to Europe with their families and the other delegates sent back to their home provinces. The news of the dissolution spread like wildfire and provoked a series of anti-imperial demonstrations, especially in the radical north-east. In Pernambuco the provincial junta refused to accept the Emperor's nominee as president and set up a rebel administration. British consuls were alarmed at the growing unrest and anxious for the safety of British communities and property, and on 2 January 1824 Sir George Eyre received an urgent message from Consul Parkinson in Recife asking for the dispatch of a British warship.[2] Fortunately the Admiral had anticipated the request and had ordered *Doris* to the north-east on 21 December to keep an eye on things. The frigate's officers therefore had only two days to savour their triumph at the Opera House before putting to sea, but seemed to welcome the break in routine. They expected to be away for only six weeks.[3]

But *Doris* was to be away for six months, not six weeks. For the first three, the frigate shuttled continuously between Bahia, Paraíba and Pernambuco as the political situation deteriorated, never spending more than four days in any one place. Writing to his brother on 16 March from the Recife roadstead, Charles Drinkwater spoke of 'poor *Doris*, continually on the move', and reflected wistfully that he had hardly been out of the ship for five days in the last three months.[4] But a major change was about to take place in *Doris*'s fortunes. A week after Drinkwater's letter, the sloop *Eclaire* appeared over the horizon carrying a new captain. The absent Captain Vernon had been superseded in his command of *Doris*, and in his place the Admiralty had appointed 26-year-old

Commander William James Hope Johnstone, captain of the *Eclaire* and son of Vice Admiral Sir William Hope Johnstone, the first naval lord at the Admiralty. Thomas Bourchier was ordered to move out of *Doris* and replace him in command of *Eclaire*.

In England Captain Vernon had been devastated to hear of his supersession, but it was largely his own fault. The courts martial of Purser Worth and Master Biddle had taken place on the *Queen Charlotte* in Portsmouth harbour under the presidency of Captain Sir William Hoste on 13 October 1823. After a day of rather nit-picking evidence, countered by a vigorous defence that private trading had always been permitted on His Majesty's ships, a slightly embarrassed court had found both men guilty of an offence under the 18th Article of War, and sentenced them to be dismissed from the service, although with a recommendation for leniency in the case of Biddle.[5] That duty concluded, Vernon had written to the Admiralty in typically ingratiating terms, explaining that he was keen to resume command of the *Doris* but, as the frigate's tour of duty was nearly over, their lordships might not think it worthwhile for him to travel all the way back to South America, and that he would 'cheerfully acquiesce' in whatever they decided.[6] Mistakenly, but understandably, the Admiralty interpreted his letter as a diplomatic hint that Vernon did not want to return and, to the Captain's distress, superseded him and put him on half pay. As for his successor, they selected the most senior officer of commander rank on the South Atlantic station, who happened – notwithstanding his youth – to be William Hope Johnstone.[7] And so, on 23 March, the new captain stood bare-headed on the *Doris*'s quarterdeck, read his Admiralty commission aloud to the assembled officers and men, and officially took charge. As usual Hope Johnstone brought with him a group of 'followers', but only seven this time – two midshipmen, Hubbard and Wakefield, a clerk called Boghurst, one seaman, and his own cook, steward and coxswain. In return Midshipman Bosanquet, Clerk Hammond and four men went with Captain Bourchier to *Eclaire*.[8] But *Doris* remained at full strength even after a two-year tour of duty. A muster taken on 21 March 1824 still showed a total complement of 245 men and boys.

The political situation in Pernambuco was also about to change, and for the worse. On 31 March two Brazilian frigates, a brig and an armed ship appeared off Recife for a showdown with the rebel authorities. All four were commanded by British officers – the *Niterói* by the *Blossom*'s old lieutenant John Taylor; the *Piranga* by Captain James Norton, ex-Royal Navy, ex-East India Company and the leader of the last contingent of officers and men recruited by the Brazilians in London in 1823; the *Bahia* by Commander Bartholomew Hayden, formerly the *Conway*'s Second Master; and the *Gentil Americana* by Lieutenant James Watson. Taylor, who was in overall command, carried secret orders. If the rebel junta refused to install the Emperor's nominee as provincial president, he was to institute a blockade. For a week there were diplomatic exchanges between Taylor and the local authorities, the latter protesting loyalty but refusing totally to obey the Emperor's commands. But by 7 April it was clear that the junta and its rebel president, Manuel de Carvalho, had no intention of submitting to Rio de Janeiro and were following the path of open rebellion. In accordance with his orders, Taylor therefore declared Pernambuco under blockade. His interpretation of his instructions was, however, liberal and, in accordance with international custom, he allowed any neutral merchantman that had sailed from its home port before the notification had arrived to pass unmolested. Thus, under *Doris*'s watchful eye, the British vessels, *James*, *Eliza*, *Passmore*, *Henry and Sarah*, *Hiram*, *Idris* and *Alexander* arrived and unloaded their cargoes in late April and early May.

The blockade dragged on for three weary months. Keeping the sea off Pernambuco during this time was no easy task for either the Brazilian blockading squadron or for *Doris*, which remained carefully on watch safeguarding British interests. The onshore winds and the reef-fringed coast were dangerous at the best of times, and the coral interspersed with white sand on the sea bed took a steady toll in anchors and cables. On 30 April a heavy swell drove the cutter against the frigate's side and smashed in its stern. The boat was repaired, but all its gear – sails, spars, oars and sails – were lost. Bad weather and heavy rain during June made the situation more uncomfortable. But as a neutral, *Doris* was able to remain in contact with the shore and continued to receive a daily ration of 230 lbs of meat, 120 lbs of vegetables and fruit, and, occasionally, a month's supply of bread, flour, sugar, vinegar, wine and brandy. But at the end of April Recife was filled with rumours that the officers on the British ships were passing on supplies to their countrymen in the Brazilian squadron. The rebel government abruptly cut off the flow of provisions. Hope Johnstone immediately protested to the provincial president, giving his assurance that the allegations were false. Manuel de Carvalho waited two weeks, then agreed that *Doris* could once again receive all the water and provisions she needed in spite of the accusations that had been made. Hope Johnstone was incensed at Carvalho's refusal to accept his word, and stiffly replied to say that the frigate would accept the offer of water, but would take no more provisions from Pernambuco and in future would rely on Bahia for supplies.[9] Meanwhile the crew fell back on the preserved beef and pork in the hold – only to find that some barrels were seriously underweight, while others were rotten and had to be thrown overboard.

Captain Hope Johnstone was politically well connected, but he was also an experienced officer, having joined as a first-class volunteer in 1811, then served in the *Adamant*, in the *Venerable* with Sir Home Popham off the north coast of Spain, and subsequently in the Channel, the Mediterranean and the West Indies. Promoted lieutenant in 1818, he had become a commander two years later and had brought *Eclaire* to South America in 1823. While *Doris* remained at her post off Recife, the new captain began to put the stamp of his personality on the ship. Unhappy with her trim, Hope Johnstone had two main deck and two quarterdeck guns moved forward to lessen her draught at the stern. The frigate was then painted from top to bottom, both inside and out. On Sundays there was divine service and mustering by divisions. Every week the lower deck was washed, and twice a week – weather permitting – clothes and hammocks scrubbed. There were now exercises with the great guns, or by the small arms men and the Royal Marines – frequently firing at a target – every ten days. Clothing was mustered, replaced or repaired every two months. And there were only two floggings, both men going to the gratings for the second time – George Moore of the Marines, given 32 lashes for insolence and disobedience, and Able Seaman James Flood, who was given 24 for drunkenness.

On 19 May, after two months of tedious and difficult duty off Pernambuco, *Doris* weighed anchor and beat out of the bay, heading for relaxation and resupply in Salvador de Bahia. But she was only able to stay for four days – long enough to water, clear the fore and after holds, and load up with six weeks' supply of bread, beef, pork, flour, raisins, sugar and brandy together with six live oxen. But at last there were letters from England. With the delay of the April packet from Rio, *Doris* had received no communication from home for two months. Now there were two mail-bags sent on from Rio de Janeiro – one handed over by the Brazilian frigate *Piranga*, the other delivered by the packet *Princess Elizabeth* on her way to England. For the officers, news from home was an additional source of excitement. The men celebrated the stay in Bahia by a drunken spree which resulted in six of them being hauled before the captain for punishment. However, this time only two were flogged – James Flood (again) and Colin Macintyre. The other four had their grog stopped for one month – the first time this sensible deterrent had been tried. In fact Hope Johnstone's punishment record during his ten months of command was the most lenient of all the *Doris*'s captains, averaging only one flogging and 30 lashes a month. According to pundits, this was probably the minimum level needed to maintain discipline and morale.

On 29 May *Doris* weighed anchor and made sail for Pernambuco. It was a stormy passage, cloudy with heavy intermittent rain and fresh south-easterly breezes. Charles Drinkwater reported that for days on end the watch came off duty soaked to the skin with little chance of drying their clothes. As the frigate tore through the grey sea with the wind on her starboard quarter, the weakness in her gear also became apparent. On the first day out two staysails were ripped to shreds. On the second, a sudden gust split the jib. On the fifth and seventh days the royals then the flying jib were blown out. And even in sight of Pernambuco a sudden squall tore the mainsail in two and hurled a seaman overboard. Fortunately

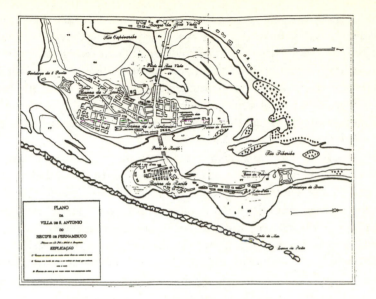

15 Recife
After Antinio Bernadino Pereira do Lago

16 The Pemambuco Junta in session, after Rugendas

the frigate was able to back her main yards and launch a boat in time to save the man from the sea. Once back in the comparative safety of the anchorage, the sailmakers and the boatswain's men sent about repairing the canvas and replacing the lost gear, while Captain Hope Johnstone complemented the exercises with the great guns and small arms with a regular programme of drills aloft aimed at speeding up the basic manoeuvres of furling, reefing, spreading and shortening sail.[10]

Meanwhile, in the British frigate's absence, the political situation in Pernambuco had sharply deteriorated. The rebel junta rejected the Emperor's attempt at reconciliation by offering a compromise candidate as president, and under Manuel de Carvalho's leadership began to suborn the neighbouring provinces and attack the imperial troops in the vicinity, raising men and arming ships for the purpose. Willy-nilly *Doris* became involved. On 22 June the Brazilian blockading squadron attacked the port in an unsuccessful attempt to cut out a rebel gunboat, leaving three defenders dead in the attempt. The rebel junta was convinced that *Doris* had helped in the assault and promptly arrested two of the frigate's midshipmen and nine men the next time a boat's crew went ashore to deliver dispatches to the consul. It took Hope Johnstone and Consul Parkinson days to secure their release and get an apology.[11] But a week later it was all over. On 28 June the blockading squadron was joined by the Brazilian schooner *Carolina* carrying new orders. And next morning when the citizens of Recife looked out to sea, the familiar white sails of Taylor's warships had disappeared. The blockade had been abandoned and the imperial squadron was on its way back to Rio de Janeiro.

In Brazil the strategic situation had changed. All through 1824, packets and warships from Europe had brought news that Portugal was gathering its military strength for an attempt at reconquest. By the middle of the year the situation appeared so serious that the Imperial Government had decided to withdraw all its military and naval forces to defend the capital. The Emperor issued a decree explaining the situation, calling on Brazilians patriotically to resist the invader, and ordering the provinces to attend to their own defence. In this emergency the blockade of Pernambuco had been abandoned.

The Brazilian Navy may have left Recife but, with British property still at risk, *Doris* had to remain. For a month Hope Johnstone and his men watched as the rebel junta became more radical and daring. Local newspapers reported the imperial decree with contempt and suspicion. The Emperor was accused of looking after his own skin, and there were dark hints that the invasion scare was a lie and that the real intention was for the Portuguese army led by the Irishman Lord Beresford to unite with the Brazilian Navy commanded by the Scotsman Lord Cochrane in order to destroy Brazilian freedom. Then, on 2 July, Manuel de Carvalho and his adherents in six adjacent provinces issued a proclamation calling for secession and the establishment of a separate republic in the north-east. It was to be called the Confederation of the Equator. This was the news that *Doris* brought back to Rio de Janeiro when, a week later, the packet *Cygnet* arrived carrying orders for her to return.

CHAPTER 15

PREPARING TO LEAVE

HMS *Doris* reached Rio de Janeiro a fortnight later. On 23 July 1824 she passed between the Sugar Loaf and the Fort of Santa Cruz, tacked her way up the Bay against a light northerly wind and let go her anchor next to the latest addition to the British South America Squadron, the 26-gun sloop *Tweed*. The anchorage was filled with merchant vessels – half of them British – and with a powerful collection of two-decked warships, each flying the flag of their respective commander-in-chief. There was HMS *Spartiate*, the French *Jean Bart*, and the Brazilian *Pedro I* with a swarm of smaller vessels of the Imperial Navy. Another 74-gun ship, the USS *Franklin*, had left only the day before for home, having been relieved in the Pacific by Commodore Hull with the frigate *United States* and the schooner *Dolphin*. As usual, the Bay was soon echoing to the thud of cannon fire as *Doris* began the customary salutes – 21 guns for the green and yellow of Brazil floating over the forts, 19 for Lord Cochrane's flag, 17 for the French Vice Admiral and 15 for Sir George Eyre. July is winter in the southern hemisphere, and the ceremonies took place on a grey sea and cloudy skies. But winter or summer, the officers and men of the *Doris* were glad to be back. As Charles Drinkwater told his father, there were 'mountains of letters to read', and they were in daily expectation of orders sending them to England. It was over three years since the frigate had left Plymouth and the whole crew knew they would be homeward bound as soon as the frigate *Blanche* arrived to relieve her.[1]

But there were no such orders awaiting *Doris* on her return to Rio. *Blanche* had not appeared, and Sir George Eyre needed every ship he could lay his hands on. From Peru there was news that the

patriot government had fallen apart, that the Spanish royalists had
regained control of most of the country including Lima and Callao,
that warships and troop convoys were on their way from Spain to
assist, and that the Peruvian Navy under its admiral, former Royal
Navy commander Martin Guise, was not only blockading the coast
but attacking the merchant ships in Callao. The situation in Brazil
was no more settled. The revolutionary turmoil in the north-east
continued, and *Doris* had brought news of an escalation of the
crisis and the establishment of a separatist republic. Fortunately
the Imperial Government was now able to throw its whole weight
against the rebels. On 30 June the packet *Sandwich* had brought
news of a counter-revolution in Portugal. The situation was
confused, but it was clear that there was now no possibility of an
attempted reconquest of Brazil. A fortnight before *Doris*'s arrival, a
Brazilian flotilla of four ships had already sailed to reimpose the
blockade of Pernambuco, and the Empire was now assembling its
military and naval forces for an all-out assault on Manuel de
Carvalho and his confederates.

The Brazilian Navy was also in a position to play its full part.
For six months it had been reeling as a result of a bitter quarrel
between Lord Cochrane and the Imperial Government over pay
and prize money. The legal and political complications of the war
of independence had been enormous, and many of Cochrane's
seizures – however audacious – were inadmissible under either
international or Brazilian prize rules. Thus it had proved impossible for the Brazilians to speedily process and condemn the
hundreds of ships that Cochrane had captured during the conflict
or pay the prize money he demanded.[2] Inevitably the First Admiral
was furious and deeply suspicious. No amount of reassurance
from the Brazilians could satisfy him, and the open quarrel caused
a drop in the Navy's morale and problems with recruitment. A
year earlier, Sir Thomas Hardy's problem had been to prevent
desertion from British ships to the Brazilian Navy. Now Sir
George Eyre had to deal with the reverse – preventing deserters
from the Imperial Navy enlisting on British ships.[3] But on 12 July
the Brazilian Government settled the quarrel in the only way
Cochrane could understand – by paying over £40,000 in hard cash

as a prize money advance to the squadron. Preparations for the expedition against the rebels were now resumed without a hitch. By the end of the month the transports were ready and a Brazilian army under General Lima e Silva had embarked. On 2 August, escorted by Lord Cochrane's flagship, *Pedro I*, a brig-of-war and a corvette, the expedition that was to bring the north-eastern rebels to heel put to sea.

Three weeks later, on 19 August, it was followed by a third squadron under the command of American-born Commodore David Jewitt in the *Piranga*, accompanied by the *Niterói* and two other warships. But this time, the *Niterói* had a new commander, Captain James Norton. After 18 months of diplomatic evasion, the Brazilian Government had been forced by remorseless British pressure to dismiss John Taylor from its service. But nothing could prevent it from showing its reluctance to take such a step and, to the discomfort of the British Consulate, when the news was announced in August, the newspapers were allowed to carry a bitter attack on British persecution of a Brazilian naval hero.[4]

The disturbances reported on both sides of the continent inevitably posed a renewed threat to British lives and property. To safeguard the situation in Brazil, Sir George Eyre promptly ordered *Tweed*, recently arrived from England as *Brazen*'s relief, to take *Doris*'s place watching over British interests in Pernambuco, while *Brazen* herself, sailing for home on 24 August, was ordered to visit Recife, Maranhão and Pará on the way in case of further trouble. In dealing with the renewed civil war in Peru, Eyre not only had three regular ships of the South America Squadron in the Pacific – the frigates *Tartar* and *Aurora* and the sloop *Fly* – but was fortunate enough to have the two-decker HMS *Cambridge* as well. *Cambridge* was one of Britain's most modern line-of-battle ships, an 82-gun giant of over 2000 tons which had been sent to the region on a 'show the flag' mission carrying the whole of the British diplomatic corps for the newly independent South American states. She had arrived in Valparaiso on 4 May 1824 via Rio de Janeiro after a dreadful voyage from Portsmouth in which her equipment had been shown to be shoddy and her puny crew inept. All three topmasts had been carried away or found to be rotten, sails had split and simple manoeuvres had been bungled, and all in full view of three consul generals, one consul and five vice consuls who, together with their families, secretaries and servants made a passenger list of over 70 persons. After emergency repairs in Rio dockyard, Captain Malling had arrived in the Pacific eager to sort out the muddle and to act as senior officer as his rank dictated. Or so he thought. The cynics in the squadron, having met his formidable wife 'Commodore' Harriot, were less sure as to who actually gave the orders.[5]

The other powers whose nationals and commerce were threatened had also increased their naval presence. Commodore Hull in the *United States* was reinforced by the sloop *Peacock*. The French sent Rear Admiral Rosamel with the frigates *Astrée* and *Marie-Thérèse* to join the *Jean Bart* and the corvette *Diligente* which were already in the Pacific. There was much fraternization between the various squadrons, the British as usual being impressed with the neatness of the French vessels and the cordiality of their officers and men, both of whom wore uniforms so like their own that the local populations were confused.[6] Acquaintance with the Americans was revealing and convivial, with the officers of *Cambridge*, *Tartar* and *Fly* invited aboard the *United States* to celebrate the Fourth of July. Surgeon John Cunningham of the *Cambridge* found the American officers not only highly professional, but showing an interest and knowledge of history, natural philosophy and science that was rare among their British counterparts. Their ships were equally impressive. The size of the *United States* in particular caused astonishment, and both Cunningham and his colleagues agreed that in her famous duel with the *Macedonian* during the 1812 war, the British ship had stood no chance. With a displacement of 1500 tons, and with 54 guns – of which 30 were main deck 24-pounders – the *United States* was found to be 'a tremendous frigate ... her scantlings throughout considerably above those of the *Cambridge* ... and her sides thicker by several inches'.[7] Indeed, one of the Americans revealed that few of *Macedonian*'s shot had managed to penetrate the vessel but had stuck in her sides like currants in a pudding.

But in dealing with the turmoil in the Pacific, Sir George Eyre

had had an extra problem to contend with. HMS *Aurora* was due
to return to England after her three-year tour of duty, and moreover was carrying tons of 'remittances' in silver from British
merchants in Peru and Chile. The political instability had made
them even more anxious than usual to get their coins and ingots
safely on board a British man-of-war. Cunningham reported that
there were 'piles of it, like shot, in the gunroom of the *Cambridge*
nearly as high as the beams. It was there cased in boxes and
afterwards put in the hold until the next ship for England took it
away.'[8] Eyre was now keen to arrange for the frigate and the
money to return round Cape Horn. *Aurora* in fact had had a lucky
escape. A year earlier, she had almost been sent north to Alaska in
search of Captain Parry. Parry had sailed from the Thames with
Fury and *Hecla* in May 1821 to look for the North West Passage
and had disappeared for two years into the ice. In September 1823
an optimistic Admiralty had decided to send *Aurora* northwards
from the Pacific to the Bering Strait to meet and assist Parry's
expedition as it triumphantly emerged from the western end of the
newly discovered Passage![9] The expedition, of course, failed in its
objective and, fortunately for Captain Prescott and his men, news
of Parry's return to England in October 1823 led to the orders
being cancelled in time.[10]

But Eyre now had to send *Aurora* home. His plan was to replace her in the Pacific with the frigate *Briton*, whose watching
brief in the River Plate would in turn be taken over by Bourchier's
sloop *Eclaire*. Unfortunately *Eclaire* was absent. The situation in
Brazil had seemed to pose a threat to the flow of provisions to
British warships, so two months earlier Eyre had sent the sloop to
the Cape of Good Hope with dispatches and his son William – on
his way to join his regiment – to see if the naval station there could
help if the situation worsened.[11] In the event, the precaution
proved unnecessary as the Royal Navy transport *Arab* arrived in
Rio stuffed with barrels of provisions and naval stores on 22 July.
But it removed *Eclaire* from the scene of the action at a crucial
time.

All this meant that *Doris* had to remain, but Captain Hope
Johnstone knew it could not be long before the frigate headed for

England and began to make preparations for the voyage. The normal daily supplies of fresh meat, vegetables and oranges had started to come aboard the moment she arrived in Rio de Janeiro. Now, on 27 July, *Doris* reprovisioned herself from the *Arab*, loading up with two months' supply of beef, pork, bread, flour, peas, vinegar and rum. Lemon juice, sugar, raisins, tobacco, cocoa and water were supplied from the shore through the British Consulate.[12] That done, the task of refitting the ship at her anchorage began. First, there were surveys of the running and standing rigging, and of the boatswain's, carpenter's and gunners' stores. Decayed and weakened items were condemned and replaced. Then the topmast and topgallant masts and yards were sent down, unrigged, checked and, if necessary, repaired or replaced. They were then swayed up again and the whole tracery of the rigging reset, tarred and blackened. With the caulkers overhauling the main decks and the boats, the frigate was then repainted from stem to stern in its livery of black and white with the help of floating stages hired from the imperial dockyard.[13]

There were also last-minute adjustments to the crew. The eight convicted smugglers who had transferred from *Spartiate* six months earlier reached the end of their five-year sentences and had to be discharged. As usual their places were easily filled by locally recruited volunteers. Acting Boatswain Williams was moved to *Brazen* on promotion, to be replaced by Boatswain Grieg of *Eclaire* when the sloop returned. Lieutenant Markham fell sick and was invalided out, but one of the flagship's senior men, John Parker – previously Hope Johnstone's First Lieutenant on *Eclaire* – was sent over to take his place and act as First Lieutenant. *Spartiate* also supplied a new commanding officer for the marines, Lieutenant Halloran, and a new surgeon, Dr Jonathan Scott. Sadly for him, the trustworthy Arthur Kift lacked the necessary certificates and could not be confirmed in the post in which he had acted for so long.[14]

By the middle of August *Doris* was ready for sea. But there were no orders for home – *Blanche* had still not arrived. Sir George Eyre decided he had no choice but to send *Doris* on one last assignment. She was to sail from Rio de Janeiro to Montevideo, carrying orders for *Briton* to leave the River Plate and to relieve *Aurora* in the Pacific. She was also to check on alarming reports that a Spanish convoy of 36 ships carrying military reinforcements to Peru had been sighted off the mouth of the River.[15] The frigate was to stay in the Plate until *Eclaire* arrived, and was then to sail direct to England. And so it was. On 27 August 1824 *Doris*'s topmen manned the yards while Sir George Eyre paid a final ceremonial visit to inspect the ship and muster the crew.[16] Then, next morning, with light winds and a cloudy sky, the frigate weighed anchor, dipped her ensign to the forts guarding the Bay, and passed through the entrance into the blue rollers of the South Atlantic.

For two weeks *Doris* sailed further and further south-west, the temperature dropping daily. On 11 September she reached the northern extremity of the River Plate, turned west, and cautiously made her through the brown waters and shallows of the estuary to where the fortified port of Montevideo lay on the northern bank 90 miles from its mouth. Next day, the frigate sighted *Briton* in the cold haze, made her number, and dropped anchor in the broad expanse of the Bay of Montevideo, the conical hill of the Cerro on its westernmost point to her left, the brick walls, towers and steeples of the city on a small peninsula to her right. *Doris* handed over *Briton*'s mail and orders, and the two ships exchanged visits and social calls. There were also some final readjustments to their crews. *Doris*'s gunroom was augmented by the addition of Midshipman Thomas Talbot for the return voyage to England, and five men from *Briton* were exchanged for three seamen and three marines who preferred to stay longer in the Pacific. One was the serial deserter Robert Campbell. His record in his new ship was no better than in *Doris*. He made one unsuccessful try to 'run' from *Briton* before disappearing at last in Valparaiso in September 1825. It had taken him four attempts.

Doris stayed off Montevideo for three weeks. There was little to do. The last Portuguese troops had evacuated the province in February, and the imperial authorities were firmly in control. Stories of the passing of the Spanish convoy were confirmed, but the number was reduced to eight transports and two warships, each easily identifiable by a loud braying of trumpets and beating of drums whenever they got under way.[17] Apart from this, there were trips ashore and the opportunity to wander round the narrow run-down streets with their whitewashed two-storey houses — gardenless, with interior courtyards in the Spanish fashion — or to gaze at the bleak treeless landscape around the town. Neither was there any joy in the weather. The River Plate was cheerless and dank at this time of the year, with the anchorage wrapped in fog or lashed by rain, and the horizon vivid with thunder and lightning. Even so, one hardy seaman still opted to desert — the first man to do so for over a year. At last, on 24 September, *Eclaire* entered the Bay, exchanging signals as she did so with HMS *Briton* finally leaving on her way to the Pacific.[18] A week later *Doris* had taken on basic provisions and water, exchanged another half a dozen men, and was gingerly heading east between the coast and the English Bank past the tiny port of Maldonado. On 7 October she turned her back on the shallow brown waters of the River Plate, leant over before the south-easterly breeze and headed into the green rollers of the South Atlantic bound for England.

CHAPTER 16

HOME AGAIN:
WINTER 1824–25

The first two days of *Doris*'s voyage home brought strong south-easterly gales and sudden squalls, laying the frigate over as she thrashed north-east under close-reefed topsails, her topgallant masts struck down to the caps. Then, for the next fortnight, she picked her way across a thousand-mile belt of variable winds, heading generally north but altering her course to cope with almost daily changes as it swung from south to south-east, to north-east then to north-west and back again. The strength of the wind varied as much as its direction. At times it rose to gale force, with *Doris* logging daily runs of up to 195 miles as she tore through the water. Twice she lost the log line overboard trying to measure the speed of her progress. At other times, there were light breezes which subsided to fitful puffs when the frigate could make no more than 25 miles a day with every stitch of canvas spread. The calms gave the chance to wash clothes, scrub hammocks and exercise the great guns or the small arms. There were even three floggings, the last of which – James Flood (for the third time), given 30 lashes on 28 October for neglect of duty – was the final act of corporal punishment to take place on *Doris* during her present commission.[1]

As the frigate headed steadily northwards, the weather became hotter, the sky clearer and the sea deeper and bluer. The men changed from cold- to warm-weather gear, discarding waistcoats and blue wool 'trowsers' for shirtsleeves and white ducks. Dolphins and flying fish appeared in the water alongside. Ten days into the voyage, on 17 October, *Doris* reached 24°S latitude and was 500 miles due east of Rio de Janeiro. For the next ten days she made only moderate progress, logging average daily runs of only 75 miles with light variable northerly and westerly winds. Then, at 20°28'S, 40°56'W, ploughing steadily north-east under a full set of canvas which included royals and studding sails, she glimpsed the distant peaks of the island of Trinidade on the horizon. The wind remained variable for a little longer; but on 1 November it began to blow steadily and with growing strength from the south-east. The frigate had reached the south-east trades.

With the trade wind now blowing steadily on her starboard quarter, *Doris* raced along under reefed topsails, topgallants and royals, picking up both speed and distance. With fine warm weather and winds varying from fresh to moderate, the frigate was able to maintain her northward heading and to cover some 180 miles a day. On 4 November, at 4°S and 650 miles due east of Brazil's farthest extremity of Cape St Roque, she logged an astonishing run of 223 miles in 24 hours. And once again she was lucky with the weather in the tropical zone. As with her outward voyage three years earlier, there were no doldrums or calms to slow her down on her return passage. The south-easterly winds continued until they had driven her well across the equator, and there were only two days of weak variables to contend with before she met the north-east trades on the other side. Then there was another week of glorious sailing as *Doris* surged into the North Atlantic, now leaning close hauled on the starboard tack with the wind forcing her only slightly westward of her northerly heading.

Mid-November found *Doris* working her way haltingly across another belt of variables. The wind again boxed the compass, swinging from east to south-west and back again, but it enabled the frigate to gain valuable distance to the eastwards. Her speed was just as unpredictable, with runs of 130 miles when the breeze freshened, alternating with as little as 21 miles when the wind weakened or died away altogether leaving her rolling in the swell. Fearing that *Doris*'s stocks of provisions – already depleted by the unexpected weeks in the River Plate – would be inadequate to cope with any delay, on 23 November Captain Hope Johnstone put the ship's company on two-thirds rations of rum, bread, flour, raisins, sugar and peas. Only beef and pork were plentiful enough to continue at the full rate. The weather was also changing with cloudier skies, squalls and occasional heavy rain. Every day the air grew colder. Officers and men changed back once more from shirts and white duck to blue woollen jackets and trousers with waistcoats. To make sure that the men were fully equipped for the northern winter, they were mustered by divisions for checks on their clothing. The purser then issued whatever cold-weather items were needed.

On 25 November *Doris* passed 34°N, 31°W and the wind began to blow more consistently from the south-west. Two days later the distant peaks of the Azores were in sight five miles to the north. The frigate adjusted her course and for the first time began to head directly for the mouth of the distant English Channel into strengthening winds, cloudy skies and an empty sea. On 1 December she had reached 43°N, 18°W and was 650 miles west of Cape Finisterre and sighted her first sail in many weeks. Then, two days later, 338 miles south-west of the Scilly Isles, running through a patch of squalls that brought rain drumming on her decks, she sighted another. It proved to be an English brig outward bound from Liverpool to Halifax. *Doris* was making good progress. But next day the wind veered and strengthened to a north-easterly gale, forcing the frigate to shorten sail, tearing a cutter from the quarterdeck davits and driving her off course towards Ireland. After 24 hours the wind dropped and backed again, enabling the frigate to head east for the mouth of the Channel. On 7 December she sighted the Lizard, altered course, and was soon making her way on a fresh, fine winter's day up past the Eddystone Lighthouse towards Portland Bill. Next day she rounded St Catherine's Point, shortened sail and came to anchor in Spithead, the grey hills of the Isle of Wight to her left, the chalk pits of Portsdown Hill ahead, and Southsea Castle on her right. Sixty-four days after leaving the River Plate, *Doris* was home.

The frigate stayed off Portsmouth for two days, bustling with the usual activity that follows a return from a foreign station. There was maintenance to carry out, letters to write, reports to be made, harbour routines to follow. Two customs officers came aboard to check manifests and cargo. The doctor pronounced the crew fit, although remarked that they all looked yellow after years in the tropics. The clerk of the cheque came aboard to muster the crew and counted a total of 235 officers and men – a ship's company of 182, 15 ship's boys, ten supernumeraries and 28 Royal Marines. Four privates and the drummer left for Portsmouth barracks the following day.[2]

On 10 December *Doris* set out for the final stage of her journey. Heading up the Channel with a cold quartering wind, she rounded Beachy Head and Dungeness, passed the cliffs and castle of Dover and, on the night of 11 December, dropped anchor in the Downs off Deal. Next day the frigate took a pilot on board, passed through the Gull Channel to the west of the Goodwin Sands, rounded the North Foreland and tacked her way westwards against a chilling wind into the Thames estuary. Next day she dropped anchor at the Great Nore, three miles from Sheerness where her journey had begun almost four years before.

But that was not the end of the story. *Doris* had been ordered to pay off in Deptford, but it was impossible to get any further up river while the strong westerly winds continued to blow. In raw, miserable weather, the frigate rolled and pitched for a week at her moorings in the Thames estuary, waiting for a change. The crew began to develop colds and chills. Then, on 19 December, Captain Hope Johnstone took advantage of a lull and change in wind direction and, using a combination of sail and the ship's boats, managed to get the frigate up as far as Gravesend. But the following day the wind swung back westerly again and stayed there. While she waited, *Doris* carried out the first stage of her decommissioning by unloading her guns and powder into hoys at Gravesend rather than at Northfleet which was usual.[3] She also took on board a Thames pilot and four officials from Customs and Excise who conducted a leisurely examination of the ship which lasted until she paid off at Deptford.[4] For a week the westerly winds continued to blow without respite. Finally, the Admiralty accepted the inevitable. At 1.15 pm on 29 December 1824, the paddle steam tug *City of London* appeared belching smoke from its tall chimneystack, took the frigate in tow and headed up river through the crowds of merchantmen, colliers, coasters and sailing barges that serviced the capital. It was only five hours before *Doris* was securely lashed alongside a hulk off Deptford Yard within sight of the copulas and white colonnades of Greenwich Naval Hospital.[5]

The stay at Deptford began on a disagreeable note. On the first day, the ship was visited by a bumptious customs supervisor called Downes who, in spite of the fact that four of his colleagues had been on board for ten days, not only re-examined every nook and cranny, but insisted on searching the officers' private baggage. Captain Hope Johnstone was incensed.[6] The next man to come on board was the clerk of the cheque who carried out a final muster of the crew. He registered 227 officers and men on board, of which 130 had formed part of the original ship's company that had taken *Doris* to Brazil four years earlier. The other 97 had either been recruited in South America or transferred from other British ships on the station.

Of the 130 members of *Doris*'s original crew, 23 were petty officers, 80 seamen and boys, 21 marines and 6 warrant officers or midshipmen – respectively Gunner Nesbitt, Schoolmaster Hyslop, Assistant Surgeon Kift, Master's Mate Forster and Midshipmen Turner and Montgomery. None of the original first-class volunteers were still on board, and the captain and the four lieutenants were all new – indeed Matthias and Drinkwater had held their ranks for only a year. What had happened to the other 115 officers and men who had sailed with *Doris* for South America four years earlier? As the muster book shows, 53 had been transferred to other ships, 40 invalided out, 13 had successfully deserted, seven had died, and two had been court martialled.[7]

With the muster concluded, the work of decommissioning began in earnest. With a full crew still on board it took no longer than four days to strike the topgallant and topmasts and yards, to unreeve the standing and running rigging, and to ferry it to the yard for storage. The anchors were then unbent and transferred ashore, together with the remaining sails, cordage and naval stores, the water tanks, and the remaining barrels of provisions. On 6 January the lower yards were struck and their rigging removed.

Then, the following day, the frigate was hauled alongside the sheer hulk so that her lower masts could be pulled like old teeth and floated into the mast pond. Less than ten days after her arrival at Deptford, *Doris* was a mastless hulk, riding light and high in the water without guns or stores. There was little left to do but take out the moveable ballast and clean the ship from stem to stern.[8] There were no visitors during this busy time. Colonel Drinkwater had been anxious to see his son as soon as he arrived, but Charles had been deeply embarrassed at the prospect of a visit by his father and sisters during the work of decommissioning. He managed to put them off by stressing the dirty nature of the work and the behaviour of the frigate's remaining livestock which, he argued, was totally unsuitable for the eyes of young ladies.[9]

With the ship emptied, cleared and cleaned, Lieutenant Halloran and his remaining 22 Royal Marines prepared to return to the barracks at Woolwich, and HMS *Doris* was officially decommissioned. On 12 January 1825 Commissioner J.D. Thompson came on board accompanied by chests of coin and notes and, with the assistance of two clerks from the Navy Board and two from the Treasury, proceeded to pay off the ship's company. The commissioned and warrant offices had been issuing bills of exchange throughout the voyage against their salaries, so the ceremony was largely a lower deck affair. The crew were mustered 'by the List', their names were read out in numerical order, and each man came smartly forward to be handed whatever wages were due to him. Only 37 of the original total of 213 marines, men and boys had given instructions that half their pay should be regularly paid to wives or dependents when they signed on, so most pocketed every penny. And since *Doris*'s voyage had lasted nearly four years, the amounts being handed over in cash were substantial. The average petty officer, able seaman and ordinary seaman went away with around £67, £56 and £42 respectively. George Ford, the ship's cook, pocketed £109 10s. Edward Penny, the man who was still first on the muster list, but had been promoted to ordinary seaman in 1822, found himself entitled to £57 4s 4d (£57.21). With deductions of 18s 8d for soap, £4 4s for slops, 13s for tobacco and £2 2s for his initial advance off the Isle of Wight, he was left with £44 4s 3d (£44.21). He took £24 4s 3d in cash and remitted the rest to be paid elsewhere at a later date. Likewise, the man who had been last on the muster list when *Doris* left Plymouth, Jonathan Bradford – since promoted to sailmaker – was entitled to a total of £90 13s 6d (£90.67). His list of deductions was, however, longer and more exotic – 8s for 'sick bay cloaths', £4 13s 3d for slops, 13s 3d for bedding (the normal charge), 4s for 'dead man's cloaths', 25s for tobacco, and £3 for 'straggling' (the minor fine for being absent without leave). Of the balance of £80 12s 8d, he took £50 12s 8d and remitted the rest. All in all, the total wage bill on 12 January 1825 was £6722, of which Commissioner Thompson and his men paid out a total of £5762 16s 4d in cash on the *Doris*'s quarterdeck. The rest was due to men who had been transferred during the frigate's tour of duty in South America and required adjustment in the various receiving ship's books.[10]

The final muster completed, the five commissioned officers were put on half pay until reappointment, and the rest of the petty officers and men were paid off and discharged ashore. But two of them were in luck. As a reward for good conduct and long service, a compassionate Admiralty on the recommendation of Hope Johnstone decided to promote Acting Master George Hingston[11] and Midshipman Turner to the rank, and half pay, of lieutenant. Turner was the only remaining Admiralty midshipman of the original batch and had frequently acted in the higher grade but had never been confirmed. Maria Graham's cousin, William Glennie, now recovered and serving in the *Samarang*, was included in the list as well. He too had acted as a lieutenant on *Doris* before his career had been cut short by illness.

The almost 'bespoke' nature of warship construction in the Napoleonic period meant that vessels often had distinct sailing characteristics and personalities which, after long periods of service, frequently generated feelings of affection and familiarity among their crews. *Doris* was a fast, seaworthy and comfortable frigate, but as they left her for the last time, few of her officers and men seem to have felt much in the way of regret. Probably the changes in her ship's company had been too frequent. The attitude of the lower deck is unrecorded, but Lieutenant Drinkwater probably reflected the attitude of the officers when he told his father that although he in no way disliked the frigate, he was tired and on the whole glad to leave.[12]

With her commissioning pennant hauled down and her ship's company discharged or transferred, *Doris* was taken into dry dock to be surveyed and repaired by the dockyard authorities. On closer inspection, the three lower masts were found to be weak and were replaced, but the hull was found to be in excellent condition. After four arduous years in the South Atlantic, the only defects that were visible were due to wear and tear – general recaulking was needed; decks, capstans, and pumps were worn and had to be replaced; and the 'copper at the water's edge wanted repair in sundry places'.[13] The fact that so little needed to be done reflected enormous credit on the Bombay shipbuilders who had built the frigate 18 years earlier. Meanwhile Lieutenant Augustus Bradshaw and a skeleton crew arrived to recommission *Doris* in the name of a new captain. A new phase in the ship's life was about to begin.

CHAPTER 17

FINAL DAYS: 1825 TO 1829

By the middle of 1825 HMS *Doris* had been recommissioned under the command of Captain Sir John Gordon Sinclair. A Scottish baronet, Sinclair was an officer of great wartime experience. Joining the Navy in 1799, he had been a midshipman on HMS *Victory* during Nelson's chase of Villeneuve to the West Indies in 1805, but had been denied participation in the Battle of Trafalgar by a posting to the frigate *Amazon*. In continuous employment in almost every part of the world after that, he had distinguished himself as commander of the corvette *Redwing* in the Mediterranean and had ended the war as a post captain. His selection for HMS *Doris* was his first appointment since the peace.

Doris had a new captain and a new crew, but her station was to remain unchanged, and by September she was back with the British South America Squadron, still under the command of Sir George Eyre. Her arrival in Rio de Janeiro coincided with the final departure of a person who had played an intimate part in the frigate's earlier commission in South America – Maria Graham. Mrs Graham had returned to Brazil a year earlier to begin a less than happy period as governess to the little Princess Maria da Glória. She had managed to make firm friends with the Empress Leopoldina but, alas, the Palace officials had conspired to freeze her out of any position of influence and after a series of disputes which had come to a head over the practice of bathing the six-year-old princess naked in front of servants and sentries, Mrs Graham had left her post. She sailed from Rio de Janeiro for the last time in a naval store ship at the same moment that HMS *Doris* arrived back in sight of the Brazilian capital.

There had been many changes while the frigate had been away.

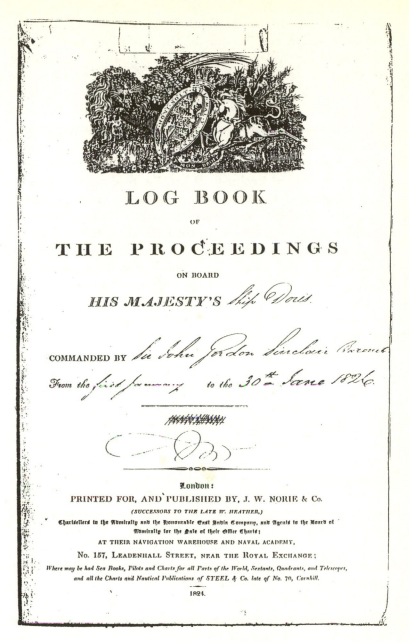

LOG BOOK

OF

THE PROCEEDINGS

ON BOARD

HIS MAJESTY'S *Ship Doris.*

COMMANDED BY *Sir John Gordon Sinclair Baronet*

From the first January to the 30th *June* 1826.

London:

PRINTED FOR, AND PUBLISHED BY, J. W. NORIE & Co.

(SUCCESSORS TO THE LATE W. HEATHER,)

Chartsellers to the Admiralty and the Honourable East India Company, and Agents to the Board of Admiralty for the Sale of their Office Charts;

AT THEIR NAVIGATION WAREHOUSE AND NAVAL ACADEMY,

No. 157, LEADENHALL STREET, NEAR THE ROYAL EXCHANGE;

Where may be had Sea Books, Pilots and Charts for all Parts of the World, Sextants, Quadrants, and Telescopes, and all the Charts and Nautical Publications of STEEL & Co. late of No. 70, Cornhill.

1824.

17 *Doris'* Log Book
Public Record Office

The war of independence had been won, and in the same month that *Doris* arrived back in Rio de Janeiro, British pressure and skilful diplomacy had not only secured a Treaty of Recognition and Peace between Brazil and Portugal, but the promise of a favourable trade agreement and anti-slave trade measures as well. At last the Empire was at peace. General Lima e Silva had successfully snuffed out the rebel Confederation of the Equator, occupying Pernambuco with his army while Recife was taken by an assault from the sea led by Captain James Norton of the *Niterói* in the absence of Lord Cochrane. When the final attack had taken place, the Admiral had been away in Salvador busily paying out prize money. Cochrane had subsequently done his bit by restoring imperial rule in the other rebel provinces but – fed up with his interminable disputes with the Brazilian Government over pay and prizes – he had then absconded to England in the frigate *Piranga*. He had arrived at Portsmouth just as *Doris* had left, and was already discussing the financial conditions of his next assignment – the liberation of Greece – this time taking the precaution of demanding his pay in advance.

But, as was usual in South America, no sooner had a dispute in one part of the continent been settled than another burst out elsewhere. This time the crisis was focused on the River Plate. In 1816 Portugal had taken advantage of the chaos reigning in the old Spanish Empire to seize the Banda Oriental – the modern Uruguay – and annex it to Brazil. Local resistance had remained dormant during the independence period, but in April 1825 the Uruguayan patriot Juan Lavalleja had raised the standard of revolt. The native population had responded with enthusiasm and before long the bulk of the province was in rebel hands while imperial control was restricted to the port cities of Montevideo and Colonia. The United Provinces of the River Plate, as Argentina was then known, rushed in with support and military help, while Brazil reinforced its garrisons and naval units. Finally, on 10 December 1825, the Imperial Government declared war.

The conflict lasted for three years. On land, Argentina and the Uruguayan patriots drove Brazil on to the defensive and steadily gained the upper hand. At sea the situation was reversed. Brazil

18 *Doris'* **entry in the Progress Book**
National maritime Museum

had a large and experienced navy and an extensive sea-borne commerce, while Argentina had tiny naval forces but an enormous international trade carried principally in British, American and French vessels. The Brazilians concentrated on strangling the trade of Buenos Aires by blockade, and on containing the audacious attacks of a small Argentinian naval squadron under the legendary Commodore William Brown. The United Provinces replied by unleashing a swarm of privateers on Brazil's sea-borne commerce. It was a messy war, fought in the shallows and mud flats of the River Plate and on the blue rollers of the South Atlantic as Argentinian privateers took on both merchant vessels and Brazilian cruisers. British and American officers and men were prominent on both sides.[1] The war ended in a stalemate and the creation of the state of Uruguay as a buffer between the two sides.

The beginning of war in the River Plate caused immediate concern to the powers whose merchant shipping was most likely to suffer disruption and interference. Independence and the abolition of the old Spanish restrictions had led to a dramatic expansion of trade in the region so that by 1825 the value of foreign goods entering the Western River Plate reached over £2 million sterling carried in 387 ships. In return, the United Provinces supplied the world with specie and with hides, tallow, jerked beef and other products of its booming cattle industry. Buenos Aires had become an international emporium, handling cottons, woollens, earthenware and clothing from Britain; lace, silks and cambric from France; wine, oil and brandy from Spain; sugar, rum, coffee and tobacco from Brazil; flour and lumber from the USA; and a miscellany of goods from other countries. Britain dominated this international kaleidoscope and in 1825 goods worth over a £1 million sterling were imported into the area in 95 British vessels. In second position, £360,000 worth of American produce arrived in 107 ships; while in third place, French luxury goods to the value of £260,000 came in the holds of 29 merchant vessels.

With war in the offing, it was no surprise that the Brazilian Navy would try to stifle this thriving trade and the revenue that Buenos Aires derived from it. The three powers that would inevitably be involved sent warships south to protect national interests. The USS *Cyane* was the only American ship on the South America station. Commanded by Captain Jesse Elliot – whose controversial career had included acting as a second in the duel which had resulted in the death of Commodore Stephen Decatur – the *Cyane* remained on lonely vigil off Montevideo and Rio de Janeiro until Congress authorized the deployment of two more warships in April 1826. The USS *Boston* arrived in June and Commodore Biddle's USS *Macedonian* in August. The French Government of Louis XVIII, always keen to fish in troubled waters, sent the brig *Faune* to watch over its interests in February, reinforced in May by Rear Admiral Rosamel with the frigates *Marie-Thérèse* and *L'Arethuse*, the corvette *Moselle*, the brig *Cygne* and the schooner *Provençale*.

The permanent strength of the British South America Squadron enabled it to take the problem in its stride. And on her arrival in Brazil, it was *Doris* that was dispatched to the Plate in October 1825 to watch over British interests and the Brazilian conduct of the blockade. The frigate remained on almost continuous watch in Montevideo for a year, reinforced temporarily by the 74-gun *Wellesley*, flagship of Sir George Eyre, the frigate *Briton* and the corvettes *Jaseur* and *Ranger*. In fact there was little for *Doris* to do. Unlike the USA and France, Great Britain recognized the Brazilian blockade and judged that with over 40 imperial warships in the river, it was both effective and lawful. As a naval power Britain was keen to ensure that the principle of strict blockade was maintained even if it resulted in the arrest of its own shipping. Only technical infringements could be challenged. And when demands for intervention from the owners of 15 British ships seized in the first year of the war began to arrive at the Foreign Office, they received a firm refusal.[2] The result was that the number of British ships sailing for the South Atlantic sharply declined and British trade fell almost to zero.

In Montevideo Sir John Sinclair and his men watched as the Brazilians slowly tightened their grip and were first-hand witnesses both to the series of daring attacks by Commodore Brown's Argentinian squadron and the vigorous response of the Brazilian blockading force, now under the command of Commodore James

Norton. There were, however, occasional trips to Rio de Janeiro to break the monotony. In June, when *Doris* returned to the River Plate, she carried Lord Ponsonby, the aristocratic grandee who had been appointed ambassador to Buenos Aires with the task of persuading the Argentinians to make peace. In October she was back in Rio to deliver dispatches and confer with a newly arrived commander-in-chief, Rear Admiral Sir Robert Otway. And in December *Doris* accompanied the Brazilian Emperor Pedro on a voyage to his army in the south carrying Ponsonby's Rio counterpart, the Hon. Robert Gordon, who had been sent out with the parallel job of getting the Brazilian to make peace.

But in January 1827 came a total change. Sir Robert Otway appointed Captain Sinclair as senior naval officer in the Pacific, and *Doris* rounded Cape Horn once more, arriving in Valparaiso on 5 March. By this time Chile and Peru had achieved complete independence. Spanish forces had been decisively defeated, their last fortresses had been abandoned and both countries were at peace. For over a year therefore, *Doris* patrolled the cities of the Pacific coast without incident, bringing reassurance to British merchants and ensuring that the supply of specie and 'freight' flowed unhindered to Great Britain. For months at a time she made Valparaiso or Callao her base, with occasional trips further north.[3]

On 18 July 1828, after one such stay, *Doris* sailed from Callao for the five-week voyage back to Chile where Sir John Sinclair expected to be relieved as senior officer by Captain Jeremiah Coghlan in the frigate *Forte*. But on the 27th day out, there was a problem. The daily sounding of the well at the foot of the mainmast showed that there were 24 inches of water in the hold. The ship was pumped dry, but next day the level increased to 36 inches.[4] *Doris* had sprung a leak. Investigations showed that the source of the problem lay in the stem of the ship above the breast hook, although little could be done while the vessel was at sea except to continue to pump. By 21 August, the frequency of pumping out the hold was increased to two then three times daily, but even so, when *Doris* reached the safety of Valparaiso nine days later and made her number to the waiting *Forte* and *Volage*, she was taking in between two and three inches of water an hour.

Neither Captain Sinclair nor his officers were unduly worried by the situation. The first survey of the damage was undertaken by Lieutenant Gretten, Master Armstrong and Carpenter Stevens of the *Volage* accompanied by Carpenter Visick of the *Forte*. It took place amid fine weather on 2 September. The hold was cleared, the water emptied from the foremost tanks and the guns were shifted aft. The effect was to tip the ship towards the stern and lift the bow by one foot, reducing her foremost draught to 15 feet 8 inches. Unfortunately the leak was still inaccessible. Two days later they tried again. Anchors, cables and chains were removed this time, the water tanks were emptied and the ship was lashed alongside the Chilean frigate *Lothario* to steady her. This raised *Doris's* bow by another foot but it was still insufficient to discover the source of the leak which seemed well below the waterline.

Over the next fortnight *Doris* was progressively lightened by removing her guns, her iron ballast, her metal water tanks, her yards, upper masts and heavy stores. This raised her bow out of the water even further and reduced her draught to 10 feet 4 inches, but still it proved impossible to reach the source of the problem, which was clearly more serious than had been thought. Eventually it was decided that there was no choice but to empty the frigate, fix huge blocks and jeers to her lower masts, and haul her over on to her side by sheer physical effort against the *Lothario* and the schooner *Montezuma* so that her keel could be examined.[5] With the assistance of the Chilean dockyard authorities and men from the other British ships in the harbour, this was done on 2 October 1828. Twenty sheets of copper were then ripped off the bow and the full extent of the damage was revealed. It could clearly be seen that the whole of the iron fastening had been eaten away in the forward part of the ship, the caulking between the timbers had decayed and there were gaps between the four strakes of planks abutting the keel through which the water was seeping.[6] Either the original protective powers of teak oil had dissipated during *Doris's* years of service, or the repairs carried out in Macao following her grounding in 1813 had been inadequate and had left her iron nails vulnerable to corrosion and worse.

Two days later the frigate was heaved down on to her side again so that more copper could be stripped off and the timbers in other parts of her bottom exposed. The examination confirmed what everyone now suspected. The official survey (the seventh) concluded that the iron nails throughout *Doris*'s hull were completely corroded, that much of her caulking was decayed and that many of the planks on her bottom strakes were decomposed. The frigate was in a bad way. It was judged that she was unseaworthy in her present state and the limited facilities in Valparaiso dockyard made it impossible to rectify the problem there.[7] On 13 October Captain Coghlan reported the situation to Sir Robert Otway, recommending that there was no choice but to abandon the ship, sell it for scrap and return the officers and crew to England in a naval transport.[8] *Doris* was then patched up, her copper replaced and her ballast, guns, gear and stores laboriously loaded back on board. There was also an extensive recaulking operation to keep the vessel afloat, carried out with the help of men not only from the *Forte*, but from the USS *Vincennes* and the French corvette *Moselle* at a cost of one dollar a day per man. By December the frigate had been watered and reprovisioned, and life had superficially returned to normal, even to the extent of regular gun drills.

In the second week of January 1829, encouraged by the fortuitous arrival in Valparaiso of two naval transports, *Kaius* and *Lord Wellington*, Captain Coghlan ordered that the *Doris* be abandoned. Over the next fortnight, the frigate was systematically stripped and emptied. The bulk of her guns, provisions, carpenter's stores, sails and cordage were transferred to the *Kaius* which sailed for Rio de Janeiro carrying half of the frigate's crew on 17 January.[9] The items that remained – mostly cordage, boatswain's stores and canvas – were sent over to other ships of the South America Squadron who happened to come into port, notably *Forte*, *Menai* and *Heron*. A week later the *Lord Wellington* became the base for the final stage of the operation and Sir John Sinclair hoisted his pennant in the transport to signify she had now become a regular ship-of-war.[10] After another fortnight the work on the frigate had been concluded. On 18 February Captain Sinclair picked up his pen and made the last laconic entry in the ship's log: 'Came on board a petty officer and a party of men and took charge of HMS *Doris*. Shifted the officers and men to the hired transport *Lord Wellington*, the *Doris* being abandoned.'[11] Then he left. A few days later the ship sailed for Cape Horn and Brazil on the first leg of a voyage that would carry Sir John Sinclair and his men to Portsmouth, discharge and half pay.

The *Lord Wellington* reached Rio de Janeiro on 23 April 1829 while, back in Valparaiso, *Doris* came under the auctioneer's hammer. Her hull, complete with lower masts, bowsprit and rigging, anchors, chain and hempen cables, her launch, pinnace and cutter, were knocked down for a total of $5590 which, after the deduction of auctioneer's fees, was exchanged to realize £1177 11s 8d (£1177.58).[12] The frigate had been launched into the waters of Bombay harbour by Sir Edward Pellew in March 1807, a credit to the skill of her Indian builders. Now, exactly 22 years later, the shipbreakers of Valparaiso came on board to take her to pieces. The life of HMS *Doris* had come to an end.

DORIS: COMMISSIONED AND WARRANT OFFICERS

August 1821

Rank	Name	Age	Eventual fate
Captain	Thomas Graham	41?	died
Lieutenants	James Henderson (a)	33?	invalided
	Charles Townsend Dance	27	promoted
	James Norbert Smart	25?	transferred to *Alacrity*
	Matthew Lys	24	invalided
Purser	Bartholomew Worth		court martialled
Master	Thomas Biddle		court martialled
Boatswain	Thomas Bond		invalided
Gunner	J. Nesbitt		completed the voyage
Carpenter	J. Oliver		invalided
Surgeon	J. Louden		invalided
Chaplain	Rev. J. Penny		resigned
Schoolmaster	James Hyslop		completed the voyage
2nd Master	George Dawes		transferred to *Morgiana*
Asst Surgeon	Arthur Kift		completed the voyage
Clerk	Henry Broughton		transferred to *Blossom*
Midshipmen	Robert Parry	19	transferred to *Blossom*
	James Brisbane	19	transferred to *Blossom*, promoted 1826
	J.H. Fitzmaurice	18	transferred to *Blossom*, promoted 1826
	Hon. F.W. Grey	15	transferred to *Conway*, promoted 1825
	J.N. Langford	16	transferred to *Conway*, promoted 1826
	Jonathan Montgomery	15	completed the voyage
Admiralty Midshipmen	C. Blatchley	25	transferred to *Briton*, promoted 1824
	James Turner	26	completed the voyage, promoted 1825

	R. Cunningham	24	transferred to *Creole*
	William Candler	24	transferred to *Alacrity*, promoted 1826
	William Glennie	24	invalided, promoted
Master's mate	Matt Forster	21	completed the voyage

August 1824

Rank	Name	Age	Date of appointment
Captain	William Hope Johnstone	26	23 March 1824
Lieutenants	John Parker		29 July 1824, ex-*Spartiate*
	Thomas Matthias	27	9 July 1823, ex-*Brazen*
	Thomas Greene	25	7 June 1823, ex-*Beaver*
	C. Drinkwater	22	2 August 1824, ex-*Briton*
Purser	J. Denis (acting)		February 1823, ex-Hardy's staff
Master	George Hingston		February 1823, ex-*Fly*
Boatswain	A. Greig		22 August 1824, ex-*Eclaire*
Gunner	J. Nesbitt		original appointee
Carpenter	William Moffat		1 May 1823
Surgeon	John Scott		25 July 1824, ex-*Spartiate*
Chaplain	———		
Schoolmaster	James Hyslop		original appointee
2nd Master	———		
Asst Surgeon	Arthur Kift		original appointee
Clerk	J.H. Boghurst		23 March 1824, ex-*Eclaire*
Midshipmen	Jonathan Montgomery	18	original appointee
	F.H. Anson	20	1 May 1822, ex-*Blossom*
	G.R. Milner	19	1 May 1822, ex-*Blossom*
	William Hubbard		23 March 1824, ex-*Eclaire*
	J.W. Noble	20	3 February 1823, ex-*Creole*
	Charles Leach	22	3 May 1823, ex-*Fly*
	J.W. Wakefield	22	23 March 1824, ex-*Eclaire*
Admiralty Midshipman	James Turner	29	original appointee
Master's mates	Matt Forster	24	original appointee
	H.J. White	21	3 May 1823, ex-*Creole*

APPENDIX 2

DORIS: PUNISHMENTS: JUNE 1821 – DECEMBER 1824

Date	Name	Rate	Lashes	Offence
(Captain Graham)				
16 Jun 1821	Oliver Martin	O	48	disobedience and insolence
18 Jul	William Vickery	AB	12	desertion
8 Aug	Laurence McAuliffe	O	48	insolence and neglect of duty
13 Aug	John Hood	AB	30	drunk and pissing on the quarterdeck
31 Aug	William Goad	O	24	neglect of duty
5 Sep	Robert Loader	O	30	skulking and neglect of duty
13 Sep	William Goad	O	36	filthiness and neglect of duty
	J. Murrill	RM	12	disobedience and insolence
27 Sep	Charles Knowling	Lm	72	drunkenness, mutinous behaviour and neglect
1 Nov	T. Clunes	RM	48	drunk on duty
	T. Cheadle	RM	24	drunk on duty
	Robert Lack	AB	24	disobedience and insolence
	William Knox	Captain MT	36	disobedience and insolence
	William Walker	AB	24	disobedience and insolence
	Thomas Frost	RM	24	disobedience and insolence
14 Nov	Thomas Harris	O	96	desertion
	Dan McAuliffe	O	96	desertion

	Silas Pinnock	AB	96	desertion
	John Williams	AB	96	desertion
	Anto Silva	O	96	desertion
	J. Flint	AB	96	desertion
10 Dec	John McNally	AB	72	leaving boat on duty
	John Buckheister	AB	24	disobedience and insolence
	William Jeffries	RM	12	disobedience and insolence
8 Feb 1822	Charles Brown	RM	54	neglect of duty and theft
18 Feb	J. Stackpole	O	12	insolence
	George Layton	RM	24	riotous behaviour
	William Sullivan	AB	42	on shore without leave
	William Crawley	RM	60	theft

(Captain Vernon)

24 May 1822	J. Sullivan	O	36	insolence
	William Stevens	AB	12	uncleanliness
29 May	John Bryan	RM	48	striking a superior officer
13 Jun	William Sullivan	AB	24	insolence
	John Bowren	AB	12	drunkenness
	John Smith	AB	12	drunkenness
19 Jun	William Lundy	O	24	drunkenness and riotous conduct
8 Jul	John Forster	AB	30	drunkenness and insolence
	William Dowling	Lm	24	drunkenness and riotous conduct
12 Jul	Charles Rodney	O	12	drunkenness
	Michael Clockeda	O	12	drunkenness
	John Moore	AB	12	drunkenness
	John Clark	Captain FT	12	drunkenness
	Dan Macdonald	O	12	drunkenness
22 Jul	John Bryan	RM	24	drunkenness
29 Jul	Edward Scott	AB	24	drunkenness
26 Aug	John Hood	AB	24	drunkenness and neglect of duty
28 Aug	William Crawley	RM	24	insolence
20 Sep	John Bowran	AB	24	drunkenness
6 Nov	Thomas Adcock	Armourer	24	drunkenness

16 Nov	John Moore	AB	24	fighting and quarrelling
20 Nov	William Leavins	O	12	quarrelling and swearing
	J. Male	Capt's cook	36	theft
6 Dec	William Flack	O	12	drunkenness and insubordination
	Mk Brown	AB	12	leaving boat
17 Dec	Dan McAuliffe	O	36	drunkenness, theft, striking the cooper
6 Jan 1823	Charles Charrock	O	24	drunkenness and disobedience
	John Clark	Captain FT	36	drunkenness and disobedience
13 Jan	J. O'Brien	O	24	drunkenness and disobedience
	John Moore	AB	24	drunkenness and disobedience
	Thomas Adcock	Armourer	12	disobedience
20 Jan	J. Stackpole	O	36	drunkenness
	Edward Scott	AB	24	drunkenness
27 Jan	William Pelham	O	18	disobedience and insolence
	William Pattisson	Captain MT	12	disobedience and insolence
15 Feb	William Knox	AB	36	out of hammock at improper time
	George Moore	RM	24	repeated neglect of duty
	Charles Charrock	O	24	drunkenness
6 Mar	J. Course	RM	24	disobedience and insolence
	James Hicks	AB	24	disobedience and insolence
3 Apr	William Crawley	RM	36	disobedience and insolence
7 Apr	William Flack	O	12	drunkenness
5 May	H. Price	AB	24	insolence and insubordination
9 May	John Moore	AB	36	repeated drunkenness
15 May	J. Bryan	RM	24	neglect of duty
6 Jun	D. Broderick	AB	12	uncleanliness
10 Jun	Mark Brown	AB	24	drunkenness
24 Jun	William Parrott	AB	24	insolence

7 Jul	Thomas Adcock	Armourer	24	drunkenness and disobedience
29 Jul	William Leavins	O	24	drunkenness and disobedience

(Captain Bourchier)

19 Aug	William Smith	AB	24	drunkenness
11 Nov	Joseph Teale	AB	24	striking a sentry
	J. Buckheister	AB	36	disobedience, attempted desertion
	J. O'Niel	RM	24	drunkenness and neglect of duty
	William Linsell	RM	36	insolence and neglect of duty
16 Jan 1824	S. Rogers	AB	12	neglect of duty
9 Feb	J. Campbell	AB	24	insolence and neglect of duty
	George Sisley	O	24	drunkenness
4 Mar	William Hancock	AB	36	contempt and neglect of duty
12 Mar	John Bowran	AB	36	repeated drunkenness

(Captain Hope Johnstone)

17 Apr	George Moore	RM	32	disobedience and insolence
20 May	James Flood	AB	24	drunkenness
31 May	James Flood	AB	36	drunkenness, quitting boat on duty
	C. MacIntyre	Captain FT	22	drunkenness
	William Leavins	O		grog stopped for 1 month for drunkenness
	Jon Steel	AB		grog stopped for 1 month for drunkenness
	William Sullivan	AB		grog stopped for 1 month for drunkenness
	James Farlane	AB		grog stopped for 1 month for drunkenness
10 Jul	John Steel	AB	24	theft
21 Jul	William Collins	AB	18	drunkenness
17 Aug	J. Bryan	RM	32	striking boatswain's mate

	Edward Penny	Lm	36	drunkenness
6 Sep	Andrew Stewart	O	36	drunkenness and riotous conduct
7 Oct	John Hood	AB	24	being below on watch
14 Oct	Pat Turner	O	16	neglect of duty
28 Oct	James Flood	AB	30	neglect of duty

Deserters fined £3 for 'straggling'

George Ford	Ship's cook
S. Pinnock	AB (twice)
Ant da Silva	O
William Johns	O
James Flood	AB
Jon Bradford	Sailmaker's crew
Dan MacAuliffe	O
William Pelham	O
Jon Williams	AB
Jon Hood	AB
Mark Johns	Captain's cook
William Harris	O
William Taylor	AB
William Bondsfield	O
William Taylor (2)	LM
Andrew Stewart	O

APPENDIX 3

DORIS: DESERTERS

Date	Name	Rate	Place
Before leaving England			
8 Apr 1821	Henry Bartlett	Boatswain's mate	Sheerness
	John Grant	Captain foretop	Sheerness
17 Apr	George Long	Lm	Sheerness
26 Apr	George Edwards	Lm	Sheerness
	William Adams	Lm	Sheerness
11 May	William Kennedy	Boatswain's yeoman	Sheerness
13 May	James Donahue	AB	Sheerness
15 May	John Williams	O	Sheerness
24 May	George Taylor	AB	Sheerness
	James Milner	AB	Sheerness
	William Cox	AB	Sheerness
	John Black	AB	Sheerness
30 May	James Chapman	O	Sheerness
	Jon Hull	AB	Sheerness
	P. Rider	Lm	Sheerness
31 May	James Sinnatt	O	Sheerness
	Josh Ellard	Lm	Sheerness
9 Jun	A. Wilkins	O	Sheerness
	M. Carter	O	Sheerness
20 Jun	George Nicholson	Coxswain of launch	Sheerness
	William Green	Sailmaker	Sheerness
21 Jun	John Roberts	Cooper	Sheerness
2 Jul	J. Thompson	Quartermaster	Sheerness
5 Jul	William Roberts	Cook's mate	Sheerness
	J. Cransdon	Boatswain's mate	Sheerness
24 Jul	John MacMullins	AB	Portsmouth
	William Dickson	O	Portsmouth
	John Macdonald	O	Portsmouth
25 Jul	James Williams	AB	Portsmouth
2 Aug	George Brown	Gunner's mate	Plymouth
After leaving England			
22 Oct	John Harrison	O	Bahia

10 Nov	L. McAuliffe	AB	Bahia
22 Nov	Robert Campbell*	AB	Bahia
19 Jan 1822	A. McKeigh	AB	Rio
21 Jan	William Myers	Gunroom cook	Rio
23 Jan	John Brown	Captain's cook	Rio
	William Walker	AB	Rio
15 May	John Williams	AB	Valparaiso
	William Bailey	AB	Valparaiso
16 May	S. Pinnock*	AB	Valparaiso
	Alex Marshall	AB	Valparaiso
18 May	J. MacNally	AB	Valparaiso
22 Aug	William Small	AB	Callao
	John Steel	AB	Callao
22 Sep	S. Pinnock	AB (second time)	Valparaiso
28 Sep	William Ward*	O	Valparaiso
18 Jan 1823	D. Macdonald	O	Bahia
8 Mar	Henry Flint	AB	Pernambuco
	Henry Curtis	O	Pernambuco
21 Mar	George Banks	Captain foretop	Bahia
	A. Stewart*	AB	Bahia
17 May	John Moore	AB	Rio
26 May	William Sullivan*	AB	Rio
28 Aug	John Lyons	Boy	Bahia
1 Sep	J. Foster	AB	Bahia
	R. Campbell*	AB (second time)	Bahia
4 Sep	William Ward	O (second time)	Bahia
2 Oct 1824	William Abercrombie	O	Montevideo

* = recaptured

DORIS: FATALITIES

Date	Name	Rate	Cause
25 May 1821	J. Gray	Boatswain's mate	natural causes
2 Jun	C. Mackey	O	falling block
19 Sep	M. Mullins	O	drowned
12 Nov	William Kyle	Carpenter's crew	natural causes
7 Jan 1822	Pat Casey	O	fell from mizzentop
27 Jan	Robert Gilles	Captain of the mast	natural causes
9 Apr	Thomas Graham	Captain	natural causes
27 Apr	F. Mack	RM	natural causes
31 May 1823	R. Harrison	AB	drowned
10 Jun	Aotaere	O	natural causes
23 Jul	James Connell	Boatswain's yeoman	natural causes
17 Nov	George Briton	AB	fell from the top
10 Oct 1824	William Collins	AB	natural causes

DORIS: RECRUITING AND RETENTION FIGURES FOR 'OTHER RANKS'

	Petty Officers	Seamen	Boys	Marines
Losses April to 12 August 1821 *(Recruits before 12 August 1821)*				
Nos recruited	**66**	**146**	**18**	**31**
Invalided out	2	11		
Ran	10	20		
Transferred	1	2		
Died	1	1		
Total	*14*	*34*		
Losses August 1821 to December 1824 *(Recruits before 12 August 1821)*				
Nos remaining	**52**	**112**	**18**	**31**
Invalided out	12	17	1	3
Ran	2	11		
Transferred	12	15	4 (+4 promoted)	6
Died	3	2		1
Total	*29*	*45*	*9*	*10*
Original crew remaining December 1824	**23**	**71 (inc 4 boys)**	**9**	**21**
Losses of those recruited/transferred August 1821 to December 1824				
Nos recruited/ transferred	**30**	**90**	**9**	**7**
Invalided out	3	2		
Ran		8	1	
Transferred	10	25	3	
Died		4		
Total	*13*	*39*	*4*	
Remaining December 1824	**17**	**51**	**5**	**7**
Total on board December 1824	**40**	**122**	**14**	**23***

*(Note: Five Royal Marines were landed at Portsmouth)

NOTES

CHAPTER 1

1. St Vincent to Directors of the East India Company, 31 March and 17 April 1802, D.B. Smith, *Letters of Lord St Vincent* (London: Navy Records Society, 1927), vol 2, pp 240–1.

2. R.A. Wadia, *The Bombay Dockyard and the Wadia Master Builders* (Bombay: K. Gurd, 1955), p 188.

3. Andrew Lambert, *The Last Sailing Battlefleet* (London: Conway Maritime Press, 1991), pp 177–8.

4. Printed in Wadia, *The Bombay Dockyard*, p 188.

5. Pellew to Marsden, 12 February 1806, NMM Greenwich, PEL/3.

6. Log of Sir E. Pellew 1805–8, PRO Kew, Adm 50/44. Letter Book 1805–7, NMM Greenwich, PEL/5.

7. *Salsette*, logs and muster books, PRO Kew, Adm 51/1698, Adm 37/1385.

8. Robert Gardiner, *Frigates of the Napoleonic Wars* (London: Chatham Publishing, 2000), p 70.

9. The movements and name changes are made clear in the logs and muster books of *Salsette*, *Pitt* and *Doris* 1805–10, PRO Kew, 51/1905, 51/1698, 51/ 1930, 51/1904, 37/ 1384, 37/1385, 37/2533.

10. Pellew to Marsden, 29 January 1806, NMM Greenwich, PEL/3.

11. Admiralty to O'Brien, 12 March 1813, National Maritime Museum, Greenwich, MKH/167. Bowen to Sir S. Hood, August 1813, NMM Greenwich, MKH/148.

12. O'Brien to Sir S. Hood, 11 December 1813, 31 March 1814, NMM Greenwich, MKH/167.

13. O'Brien to Sir S. Hood, 27 November 1813, 6 April, 11 April 1814, NMM Greenwich, MKH/167.

14. Report on sailing qualities of HMS *Doris*, 31 March 1822, PRO Kew, Adm 95/50, folio 79. This document is the source of all information on the frigate's dimensions and armaments.

15. Progress Book, vol 6, part II, NMM Greenwich, Adm 180.

CHAPTER 2

1. Chilean Navy List 1820.

Ship	Rate	Origin
O'Higgins	56-gun frigate	Spanish *Maria Isabel*
San Martin	60-gun frigate	East India Company *Cumberland*
Lautero	60-gun frigate	East India Company *Windham*
Independencia	26-gun corvette	US-built *Curiatii*
Chacabuco	18-gun corvette	local purchase
Galvarino	18-gun brig	HMS *Hecate*
Araucano	16-gun brig	American *Colombia*
Pueurredon	14-gun brig	local purchase, ex-*Aguila*
Potrillo	7-gun brig	formerly Spanish
Montezuma	5-gun schooner	local purchase

2. Donald J. Cubbitt, 'The Manning of the Chilean Navy', in *Mariner's Mirror*, vol 63, no 2, May 1977, pp 115–27.

3. Pilar C. Manrubia, *La Marina de Guerra Española en el Primer Tercio del Siglo XIX* (Madrid: Editorial Naval, 1992), p 120; annexed report, p 309.

4. Bowles to Croker, 28 November 1817, PRO Kew, Adm 1/23.

CHAPTER 3

1. R.A. Humphries, *British Consular Reports on the Trade and Politics of Latin America* (London: Royal Historical Society, 1940).

2. Bowles to Croker, 21 December 1818 and 15 March 1819, PRO Kew, Adm 1/24; Hardy to Croker, 26 June and 15 August 1821, PRO Kew, Adm 1/24 and 1/26, all printed in R.A. Graham, *The Navy and South America* (London: Navy Records Society, 1962), pp 257, 263, 339 and 345.

3. Hardy to Croker, 12 December 1821, PRO Kew, Adm 1/27.

4. J.B. Hedderwick, *The Captain's Clerk* (London: Hutchinson, 1957), p 117.

5. *ibid.*, pp 177–8.

6. Hardy to Brown, 30 August 1823, PRO Kew, Adm 1/28.

7. J.B. Hedderwick, *The Captain's Clerk*, p 131.

8. Hardy to Croker, 8 September 1822, PRO Kew, Adm 1/27; Hall to Hardy, 31 August 1822, PRO Kew, Adm 1/1864.

9. Hardy letter of 29 November 1821, printed in Broadly and Bartelot, *Nelson's Hardy – The Life and Letters of Sir T Hardy* (London: John Murray, 1909), p 186.

10. Hardy letter of 22 October 1822, *ibid.*

11. E.B. Billingstay, *The US Navy and the Wars of Independence in Chile and Peru* (Chapel Hill: University of North Carolina, 1967), p 145.

12. Basil Hall, *Extracts from a Journal Written on the Coasts of Chile, Peru and Mexico, 1820, 1821 and 1822* (Edinburgh: Constable, 1824), vol 1, entry for 16 January 1820.

13. Hardy to Croker, 23 October 1820, PRO Kew, Adm 1/26.

CHAPTER 4

1. See Richard Hill, *The Prizes of War* (Stroud: Sutton for RN Museum Publications, 1998), pp 177–8, 184–5.

2. Pay book of HMS *Doris*, PRO Kew, Adm 35/4092.

3. 'Captain Marryat on the Disposition of a Ship's Company', in J.S. Bromley (ed), *Manning Pamphlets* (London: Navy Records Society, 1974), pp 347–51.

4. Captain's log of HMS *Doris*, PRO Kew, Adm 51/3147.

5. J. Burnett, *Plenty and Want; A Social History of Food from 1815 to the Present* (London: Routledge, 1985), pp 28, 40.

6. William Cobbett, *Rural Rides* (1830), and James P. Kay, *The Moral and Physical Condition of the Working Class Employed in the Cotton Manufacture in Manchester* (1832).

7. Printed in J. Burnett, *Plenty and Want*, p 53.

8. John D. Byrn Jnr, *Crime and Punishment in the Royal Navy: Discipline in the Leeward Island 1784–1812* (Aldershot: Scolar, 1989).

9. N.A.M. Rodger, 'Stragglers and Deserters from the Royal Navy during the Seven Years' War', *Bulletin of the Institute of Historical Research*, no 57, p 67.

10. N.A.M. Rodger, *The Wooden World* (London: Fontana, 1986), p 227.

11. Tables in *English Historical Documents XI, 1783–1832* (London: Eyre and Spottiswood, 1959), p 551.

12. Report on debate of 9 January 1825, in *English Historical Documents XI*, p 881.

13. John D. Byrn Jnr, *Crime and Punishment*, pp 225–8.

14. Dudley Pope, *The Black Ship* (London: Weidenfeld and Nicholson, 1963), p 335–7.

15. Captain's log of HMS *Doris*, PRO Kew, Adm 51/3147.

16. *ibid.*

17. Hardy to Graham, 12 May 1822, PRO Kew, Adm 50/146.

18. Admiralty to Hardy, 27 July 1822, PRO Kew, Adm 50/146.

19. E. James, *Life of Commander Henry James RN* (London: Spottiswood, 1899), p 56.

20. Surgeon's log of HMS *Blossom* 1822–4, PRO Kew, Adm 101/91-3.

CHAPTER 5

1. Progress Book, vol 6, part II, NMM Greenwich, Adm 180.

2. These and other details of day-to-day activity, supplies and routine are drawn from the Captain's log of HMS *Doris*, PRO Kew, Adm 51/3147.

3. These can be found in PRO Kew, Adm 1/5467.

4. Quoted in Rosamond B. Gotch, *Maria, Lady Callcott, the Creator of 'Little Arthur'* (London: Murray, 1937), p 183.

5. Admiralty to Port Admirals, 12 March 1818, PRO Kew, Adm 2/1254.

6. See *Navy Lists* for 1821 to 1827. The following shows the proportions of Admiralty midshipmen carried in relation to the total number of midshipmen/master's mates:

Ship	Total	Admiralty midshipmen
Conway	13	8
Brazen	14	11
Superb	38	13

Briton	11	3
Blossom	11	7
Creole	16	8
Doris	12	5
Aurora	10	6

The full picture is difficult to see as ships 'rated' some Admiralty midshipmen as 'inferior' warrant officers. Muster books of ships quoted, PRO Kew.

7. Graham to Croker, March to May 1821, PRO Kew, Adm 1/1864.

8. *ibid.*

9. *Aurora*, a frigate of similar size, did slightly better. She only lost 20 men through desertion before sailing. The fact that she was re-fitting at Chatham, where a supply of reliable and experienced men were more easily available than in the distant mudflats of Sheerness, may help to explain the difference. However, *Blossom*, a sloop of the South America Squadron preparing at Portsmouth with a ship's company of 110, lost 14 men; and the brig *Beaver* with a crew of 65 lost five. *Doris*'s desertion rate seems to be about par for the course. PRO Kew, Adm 37/6536, 37/6634, 37/6631 and 37/6547.

10. These and other details of the ship's company in this chapter are drawn from the muster book of HMS *Doris*, PRO Kew, Adm 37/6547.

11. Quoted in Gotch, *Maria, Lady Callcott*, p 183.

12. *ibid.*, p 184.

13. Graham to Croker, 27 July 1821, PRO Kew, Adm 1/1864.

14. Muster book of HMS *Doris*, PRO Kew, Adm 35/6547.

CHAPTER 6

1. Captain's log of HMS *Doris*, PRO Kew, Adm 51/3147.

2. *ibid.*, entries for 16 June, 18 July, 8 and 13 August 1821.

3. *ibid.*, 21 August 1821.

4. Maria Graham, *Journal of a Voyage to Brazil and Residence There during Part of the Years 1821, 1822 and 1823* (London, 1824; reprinted New York: F. A. Preager, 1969), p 80.

5. *ibid.*, p 88.

6. Captain's log of HMS *Doris*, PRO Kew, Adm 51/3147, Sept 1821.

7. *ibid.*, 31 August, 5 September, 13 September 1821.

8. Maria Graham, *Journal of a Voyage to Brazil*, p 93.

9. *ibid.*, p 91.

CHAPTER 7

1. Maria Graham, *Journal of a Voyage to Brazil*, p 103.

2. *ibid.*, pp 118–19.

3. *ibid.*, pp 112, 121.

4. Captain's log of HMS *Doris*, October–November 1821, PRO Kew, Adm 51/3147.

5. Graham to Hardy, 14 October 1821, PRO Kew, Adm 1/1864.

6.   Captain's log of HMS *Doris*, entry for 5 October 1821, PRO Kew, Adm 51/3147.

7.   Maria Graham, *Journal of a Voyage to Brazil*, p 125.

8.   A model of this vessel, the *Constituição*, which was launched a year later, can be seen in the National Maritime Museum, Greenwich.

9.   Maria Graham, *Journal of a Voyage to Brazil*, pp 135, 142.

10. *ibid.*, p 153.

11. Captain's log of HMS *Doris*, October–November 1821, PRO Kew, Adm 51/3147.

12. Maria Graham, *Journal of a Voyage to Brazil*, p 156.

13. Drinkwater to his father, 20 October 1820, NMM Greenwich, DKW/2.

14. Captain's log of HMS *Doris*, 14 November 1821, PRO Kew, Adm 51/3147.

15. Muster book of HMS *Doris*, PRO Kew, Adm 37/6547.

CHAPTER 8

1.   Maria Graham, *Journal of a Voyage to Brazil*, p 186.

2.   Captain's log of HMS *Doris*, November 1821–February 1822, PRO Kew, Adm 51/3147.

3.   *ibid.*

4.   Maria Graham, *Journal of a Voyage to Brazil*, pp 159–64.

5.   *ibid.*, p 189.

6.   *ibid.*, p 167.

7.   Muster book of HMS *Slaney*, PRO Kew, Adm 37/6472.

8.   Hardy letter of 6 October 1822, printed in Broadly and Bartelot, *Nelson's Hardy – The Life and Letters of Sir T Hardy*, p 191.

9.   Maria Graham, *Journal of a Voyage to Brazil*, p 200.

10. Captain's log of HMS *Doris*, February–March 1822, PRO Kew, Adm 51/3147.

11. Captain's log of HMS *Doris*, 16 March 1822, PRO Kew, Adm 51/3147.

12. Maria Graham, *Journal of a Voyage to Brazil*, pp 202–5.

13. *ibid.*

14. Captain's log of HMS *Doris*, 8 April 1822, PRO Kew, Adm 51/3147; and Henderson to Hardy, 28 May 1822, PRO Kew, Adm 50/146.

15. Maria Graham, *Journal of a Residence in Chile during the Year 1822* (New York: F.A. Praeger, 1969), p 210.

CHAPTER 9

1.   William O'Byrne, *Naval Biographical Dictionary* (London: John Murray, 1848), vol 2.

2.   E. James, *Life of Commander Henry James*, p 60.

3.   Muster books of HMS *Doris* and *Blossom*, PRO Kew, Adm 37/6547 and 37/6634.

4.   Henderson to Croker, 28 April 1822, PRO Kew, Adm 1/2947.

5.   Hardy to Graham, 28 March 1822, PRO Kew, Adm 50/145.

6.   Hardy to Hall, 16 December 1821, PRO Kew, Adm 50/145.

7. Hardy to Croker, 8 September 1822, PRO Kew, Adm 1/27.

8. Basil Hall, *Extracts from a Journal*, entry for 5 May 1822. Hall to Hardy, 8 and 31 August 1822, PRO Kew, Adm 1/1857.

9. Hardy to Croker, 15 July 1822, PRO Kew, Adm 1/27.

10. Muster book of HMS *Doris*, PRO Kew, Adm 37/6547.

11. Hardy to Croker, 8 September 1822, PRO Kew, Adm 1/27.

12. *ibid.*

13. Vernon to Croker, 26 November 1823, PRO Kew, Adm 1/2634.

14. Between August 1822 and July 1823 there were 34 floggings on *Doris* involving 26 different men. The total number of lashes was 810. All the details of routine, exercises, punishments etc can be found in the Captain's log of HMS *Doris*, PRO Kew, Adm 51/3147.

15. *ibid.*, entry for 16 September 1822.

16. J.B. Hedderwick, *The Captain's Clerk*, p 125.

17. Hardy to Croker, 4 February 1823, PRO Kew, Adm 1/28.

18. Maria Graham, *Journal of a Residence in Chile*, for all her adventures in Chile.

19. *ibid.*, pp 277–8. Vernon to Hardy, 22 November 1822, PRO Kew, Adm 1/2634.

20. J.B. Hedderwick, *The Captain's Clerk*, p 106.

21. Receipts for a total of $16,997 ($8500 originally to *Alacrity* plus $8497 to *Doris*) in Dundonald Papers, Scottish Record Office, Box 7/262.

CHAPTER 10

1. See Brian Vale, *Independence or Death!: British Sailors and Brazilian Independence 1822–25* (London: I.B. Tauris, 1995) for the whole story.

2. Hardy to Croker, 29 October 1822, no 114, PRO Kew, Adm 1/27.

3. Hardy to Hall, 14 October 1822, PRO Kew, Adm 50/146.

4. Captain's log of HMS *Doris*, February 1823, PRO Kew, Adm 51/3147.

5. *ibid.*

6. All these changes can be traced in *Doris*'s muster book, PRO Kew, Adm 37/6547.

7. Hardy to Croker, no 17, 9 February 1823, PRO Kew, Adm 1/28. Quotation from Hardy to Chamberlain, 25 September 1822, Portsmouth Naval Museum, 84/347 (1–19).

8. Maria Graham, *Journal of a Voyage to Brazil*, p 247.

9. Vernon to Hardy, 2 February 1822, PRO Kew, Adm 50/145.

10. Hardy to Croker, 6 February 1823, nos 14 and 15 with annexes; Admiralty minute of 1 April 1823, PRO Kew, Adm 1/28 and Adm 50/146.

11. Hardy to Croker, no 121, 5 November 1822, PRO Kew, Adm 1/27.

12. Hardy to Croker, no 17, 9 February 1823, PRO Kew, Adm 1/28.

13. Hardy to Croker, no 21, 9 March 1823, PRO Kew, Adm 1/28. Consul-General Chamberlain to FO, 6 February, 8 April, 5 July 1823, PRO Kew, FO 63/260–1.

CHAPTER 11

1. Sir T. Hardy's journal entries for April 1823, PRO Kew, Adm 50/146; Vice Consul Follett (Bahia) to Canning 29 April 1823 (with annexes), PRO Kew, FO 63/263.
2. Captain's log of HMS *Doris*, March–April 1823, PRO Kew, Adm 51/3147.
3. Muster book of HMS *Doris* for all these details, PRO Kew, Adm 37/6547.
4. Captain's log of HMS *Doris*, 24, 27, 28 May 1823, PRO Kew, Adm 51/3147.
5. José Bonifácio to Chamberlain, 28 May and 7 June 1823, *Archivo Diplomático da Independência*, vol II (Rio de Janeiro, 1922). Chamberlain to Hardy, 30 May and 9 June 1823, PRO Kew, Adm 1/28.
6. Hardy to Chamberlain, 21 June 1823, PRO Kew, Adm 50/146. Hardy to Croker, no 77, 31 July 1823, Adm 1/28.
7. Hardy to Croker (with annexes), no 77, 31 July 1823, PRO Kew, Adm 1/28.
8. E. James, *Life of Commander Henry James RN*, p 60.
9. Hardy to Brown, 10 June 1823, annexed to Hardy to Croker, no 100, 20 September 1823, PRO Kew, Adm 1/28.
10. Maria Graham, *Journal of a Voyage to Brazil*, pp 263–73; 300–6.
11. Muster book of HMS *Doris* for all these details, PRO Kew, Adm 37/6547. Of the 83 'missing' members of the ship's company, 27 had been invalided, 27 transferred, 14 had deserted, and five had died.
12. Hardy to Croker, nos 82 and 87, 3 and 5 August 1823, PRO Kew, Adm 1/28.
13. Muster book of HMS *Beaver*, Vernon to Croker, 22 November 1823, PRO Kew, Adm 37/6631, Adm 1/2634.
14. Hardy's journal entry for 4 August 1823, PRO Kew, Adm 50/146.

CHAPTER 12

1. Basil Hall, *Extracts from a Journal*, vol 2, p 160.
2. Captain Robert Eliot to Colonel Drinkwater, 11 November 1820, NMM Greenwich, DKW/2.
3. Muster book of HMS *Superb*, PRO Kew, Adm 37/6326. Likewise the sloops *Conway* (26) and *Blossom* (24) which had establishments of six midshipmen/master's mates, carried 13 and 11 respectively; while the frigates *Brazen* (42) and *Creole* (46) with establishments of eight had 14 and 16 midshipmen/master's mates on board. PRO Kew, Adm 37/6420, Adm 37/6634, Adm 37/7059, and Adm 37/6343.
4. Hardy to Colonel Drinkwater, 18 June 1822, NMM Greenwich, DKW/2.
5. Hardy letter to his brother, 9 July 1820, printed in Broadly and Bartelot, *Nelson's Hardy*, p 183.
6. Roger Morriss, *Cockburn and the British Navy in Transition* (Exeter: University of Exeter, 1997), p 177.

7. Hardy letters of 1 January 1822 and 3 July 1823, Broadly and Bartelot, *Nelson's Hardy*, and NMM Greenwich, MS/89/0440.

8. Admiralty letter no 33, received 6 December 1821, PRO Kew, Adm 50/145.

9. The 21 'veteran' promotees were Messrs Anderson,* Austin,* Becher, Best,* Blake,* Blatchley, Clay, Dixon, Frampton, Gilly, Greene, Grove, Liddell, Mansfield, Matthias, Morris, Parlby, Poynter, Rawden, Sheringham and Teek (*designates a Hardy 'follower'). I am indebted to Ann Savours for the information on Horatio Austin. Hardy's Dorset 'friends' comprised Midshipmen Cox and Williams, and Clerks Ward and Thorne.

10. Hardy to Colonel Drinkwater, 2 November 1822, NMM Greenwich, DKW/2.

11. Hardy to Colonel Drinkwater, 18 June 1822, NMM Greenwich, DKW/2.

12. See Brian Vale, *Independence or Death*, pp 21–2.

13. See also Brian Vale, *'A War Betwixt Englishmen': Brazil versus Argentina in the River Plate, 1825–30* (London: I.B. Tauris, 2000).

14. C. Drinkwater to his father, 18 June 1822, NMM Greenwich, DKW/2.

15. See Porter's entry in O'Byrne, *Naval Biographical Dictionary*.

16. C. Drinkwater to his father, 5 August 1823, NMM Greenwich, DKW/2.

CHAPTER 13

1. Maria Graham, *Journal of a Voyage to Brazil*, p 264.

2. Chamberlain to FO, no 112, 18 September 1823, Hardy to Croker, 29 September 1823, PRO Kew, FO 63/260 and Adm 1/28.

3. Hardy Order of 22 August 1823, PRO Kew, Adm 1/146.

4. Hardy to Willes, 10 June 1823, PRO Kew, Adm 1/28.

5. Hardy to Bourchier, 11 August 1823, PRO Kew, Adm 50/146.

6. Hardy to Brown, 30 August 1823, PRO Kew, Adm 1/28.

7. Hardy to Hope Johnstone, 5 September 1823, PRO Kew, Adm 1/28.

8. Hardy to Croker, 20 September 1823, PRO Kew, Adm 1/28.

9. Muster book of HMS *Doris*, PRO Kew, Adm 37/6547.

10. Captain's log of HMS *Doris*, August–September 1823, PRO Kew, Adm 51/3147.

11. *ibid*.

12. Maria Graham, *Journal of a Voyage to Brazil*, p 320–3.

13. Eyre's journal entry for 18 November 1823, PRO Kew, Adm 50/147.

14. Captain's log of HMS *Doris*, 25 November 1823, PRO Kew, Adm 51/3147.

CHAPTER 14

1. Drinkwater to his sister, 27 December 1823, NMM Greenwich, DKW/2.

2. Eyre's journal, 2 January 1824, PRO Kew, Adm 50/147.

3. Drinkwater to his father, 9 January 1824, NMM Greenwich, DKW/2.

4. Drinkwater to his brother, 16 March 1824, NMM Greenwich, DKW/2.

5. Court Martial Reports, PRO Kew, Adm 1/5467.

6. Vernon to Croker, 16 October 1824, PRO Kew, Adm 1/2634.

7.   Admiralty note attached to the above.

8.   Captain's log of HMS *Doris*, 23, 24 March 1824, PRO Kew, Adm 51/3147.

9.   Correspondence of Hope Johnstone to Carvalho, 29 April and 9 May 1824, PRO Kew, Adm 1/1957.

10. These and other details are to be found in the Captain's log of HMS *Doris*, PRO Kew, Adm 51/ 3147.

11. Hope Johnstone to Eyre (with enclosures), 30 June 1824, PRO Kew, Adm 1/1957.

CHAPTER 15

1.   Drinkwater to his father, 2 August 1824, NMM Greenwich, DKW/2.

2.   Brian Vale, *Independence or Death*, pp 99–108.

3.   Eyre to Croker, no 8, 9 January 1824, PRO Kew, Adm 1/29.

4.   Chamberlain to Canning, no 95, 22 Aug 1824, PRO Kew, FO 63/278.

5.   John Cunningham, *Remarks During a Voyage to the Pacific 1823–55* (unpublished manuscript), NMM Greenwich, JOL/21. See also E. James, *Life of Commander Henry James*.

6.   *ibid.*

7.   John Cunningham, *Remarks During a Voyage*.

8.   *ibid.*

9.   Barrow to Eyre, 8 September 1823, PRO Kew, Adm 3/262, quoted in Barry Gough, *To the Pacific with Beechey: The Journal of Lieutenant George Pearce of HMS Blossom, 1825–8* (Cambridge: Cambridge University Press for the Hakylut Society, 1973).

10. Eyre to Brown, 14 February 1824, PRO Kew, Adm 50/147.

11. Eyre to Bourchier, 7 June 1824, PRO Kew, Adm 50/147.

12. Captain's log of HMS *Doris*, 27 July to 26 August 1824, PRO Kew, Adm 51/3147.

13. *ibid.*

14. Muster book of HMS *Doris*, PRO Kew, Adm 37/6547.

15. Eyre to Croker, no 75, 31 October 1824, PRO Kew, Adm 1/29.

16. Captain's log of HMS *Doris*, 27 August 1824, PRO Kew, Adm 51/3147.

17. Eyre to Croker, no 75, *ibid.*

18. Captain's log of HMS *Doris*, 24 September 1824, PRO Kew, Adm 51/3147.

CHAPTER 16

1.   Details of the voyage from Captain's log of HMS *Doris*, October to December 1824, PRO Kew, Adm 51/3147.

2.   Muster book of HMS *Doris*, PRO Kew, Adm 37/6551.

3.   Hope Johnstone to Croker, 29 December 1824, PRO Kew, Adm 1/1957.

4.   Muster book of HMS *Doris*, PRO Kew, Adm 37/6551.

5.   Captain's log of HMS *Doris*, 29 December 1824, PRO Kew, Adm 51/3147.

6.   Hope Johnstone to Croker, 30 December 1824, PRO Kew, Adm 1/1957.

7. Muster book of HMS *Doris*, PRO Kew, Adm 37/6547–6551. Recruiting and retention figures for 'other ranks' were as given in Appendix 5.

8. Captain's log of HMS *Doris*, January 1825, PRO Kew, Adm 51/3147.

9. Drinkwater to his father, 11 December 1824, NMM Greenwich, DKW/2.

10. Pay book of HMS *Doris* for all these details, PRO Kew, Adm 35/4092.

11. Hope Johnstone to Croker, 30 December 1824, PRO Kew, Adm 1/1957.

12. Drinkwater to his father, 9 December 1824, NMM Greenwich, DKW/2.

13. Deptford Yard to Navy Board, 1 to 20 January; 10 March 1825, PRO Kew, Adm 106/2344.

CHAPTER 17

1. For the story of the naval war see Brian Vale, *A War Betwixt Englishmen*.

2. Correspondence between Canning and British ship owners, August to September 1826, PRO Kew, FO 6/19.

3. Captain's log of HMS *Doris* for 1827, PRO Kew, Adm 51/3148.

4. *ibid.*, 18–20 August 1828.

5. Survey Report no 4, given in Captain's log of HMS *Doris*, 8 September 1828. Coghlan to Otway, 12 September 1828, PRO Kew, Adm 50/158.

6. Survey Report no 5, given in Captain's log of HMS *Doris*, 2 October 1828, *ibid.*

7. Survey Report no 7 given in Captain's log of HMS *Doris*, 8 October 1828, *ibid.*

8. Coghlan to Otway, 13 October 1828, PRO Kew, Adm 50/158.

9. Captain's log of HMS *Doris*, 17 October 1828. Coghlan to Otway, 18 January 1829, PRO Kew, Adm 50/158.

10. Coghlan to Sinclair, 26 January 1829, enclosed in Sinclair to Croker, 16 Aug 1829, PRO Kew, 1/2557.

11. Captain's log of HMS *Doris*, 18 February 1829, PRO Kew, Adm 50/3148.

12. Progress book, vol 6, part 2, NMM Greenwich, Adm 180.

BIBLIOGRAPHY

PRIMARY (in Public Record Office unless otherwise stated)

Commander-in-chief's journals
Sir E. Pellew 1805–8, Adm 50/44
Sir T. Hardy 1821–23, Adm 50/145–6
Sir G. Eyre 1823–26, Adm 50/147–8
Sir R. Otway 1826–29, Adm 50/158

Commander-in-chief's letters
Sir E. Pellew 1805–8, NMM Greenwich, PEL/3 and /5
Sir W. Bowles 1819–21, Adm 1/23–4
Sir T. Hardy 1821–23, Adm 1/25–8
Sir G. Eyre 1823–26, Adm 1/29
Sir R. Otway 1826–29, Adm 1/31

Documents from HMS *Doris*
Pay book, Adm 35/4092
Captain's log, Adm 51/3147
Master's log, Adm 52/4083
Muster books, Adm 37/6547–6551
Captain's log (1827), Adm 51/3148

Documents from other ships

Muster books:
Salsette, Pitt, Doris, 1805–10, Adm 37/1384, Adm 37/1385, Adm 37/2533
Aurora, Adm 37/6536
Alacrity, Adm 37/6622
Blossom, Adm 37/6634
Beaver, Adm 37/6631
Brazen, Adm 37/6326
Briton, Adm 37/6926
Conway, Adm 37/6420
Creole, Adm 37/6343
Eclaire, Adm 37/7097
Owen Glendower, Adm 37/6367

Slaney, Adm 37/6472
Superb, Adm 37/6326
Tartar, Adm 37/7010

Captains' logs:
Salsette; Pitt; Doris, 1805–10, Adm 51/1905, Adm 51/1718; Adm 51/1904, 1698;
    Adm 51/ 1930
Tweed, and *Conway*, NMM Greenwich, HTN/1 and MLM/101/2

Captains' letters (by initials of officer's surname):
B = Adm 1/1570
D = Adm 1/1745
G = Adm 1/1864
H = Adm 1/1957
S = Adm 1/2557
V = Adm 1/2634

Lieutenants' letters (by initials of officer's surname):
D = 1/286
H = 1/2947
L = 1/3151
S = 1/299

Others
Archivo Diplomático da Independência, Ministério de Relações Exteriores, Rio de
    Janeiro, 1922
Correspondence, Rio de Janeiro to Foreign Office 1823–24, FO 63/258–61;
    63/276–79
Court Martial Reports (1823), Adm 1/5467
Cunningham, John, *Remarks during a Voyage to the Pacific 1823–5* (unpublished
    manuscript), NMM Greenwich, JOL/21
Deptford Yard Letter Book, to Navy Board, Adm 106/2344
Drinkwater Papers, NMM Greenwich, DKW/2
Correspondence of Captains O'Brien and Bowen with Sir S. Hood 1813–14,
    NMM Greenwich, MKH/167 and MKH/148
Hardy letters, Portsmouth Naval Museum, 84/347 (1–19); NMM Greenwich MS
    89/044, MS 43/73
Instructions to C-in-Cs: Hardy, September 1819, Adm 2/1328; Eyre, August
    1823, Adm 2/1328
Letters re midshipmen, Adm 2/1254, 2/1622
Lieutenants' Passing Certificates, Adm 107/45–55
Midshipmen/Masters' mates Succession Books, 1822–28, Adm 11/25
Movement of ships (East Indies), Adm 7/558
Progress Book *(Doris* entry), vol 6, part II, NMM Greenwich, Adm 180
Sheerness letters, Adm 106/91–3, Adm 106/1851
Trials and Sailing Tests of *Doris*, Adm 95/50, folio 79
Surgeon's log, HMS *Blossom* 1822–4, Adm 101/91–3

Secondary

Bartlett, C. P., *Great Britain and Sea Power, 1815–1853* (Oxford: Clarendon, 1963)

Billingstay, Edward B., *The US Navy and the Wars of Independence in Chile and Peru* (Chapel Hill: University of North Carolina, 1967)

Broadly and Bartelot, *Nelson's Hardy – The Life and Letters of Sir T Hardy* (London: John Murray, 1909)

Burnett, J., *Plenty and Want; A Social History of Food from 1815 to the Present* (London: Routledge, 1985)

Byrn, J.D., *Crime and Punishment in the Royal Navy. Discipline on the Leeward Islands Station 1784–1812* (Aldershot: Scolar, 1989)

Cubbitt, Donald J., 'The Manning of the Chilean Navy', *Mariner's Mirror,* May 1977, pp 115–27

English Historical Documents XI, 1783–1832 (London: Eyre and Spottiswood, 1959)

Gardiner, Robert, *Frigates of the Napoleonic Wars* (London: Chatham Publishing, 2000)

Gotch, Rosamond B., *Maria, Lady Callcott, the Creator of 'Little Arthur'* (London: Murray, 1937)

Gough, Barry M., 'Sea Power and South America. The Brazils S America Station 1808–1837', *American Neptune*

Gough, Barry M., *To the Pacific with Beechey: The Journal of Lieutenant George Pearce of HMS Blossom, 1825–8* (Cambridge: Cambridge University Press for the Hakluyt Society, 1973)

Gough, Barry M., 'Specie conveyance from the West Coast of Mexico in British Warships, 1820–70', *Mariner's Mirror,* vol 69, 1983, pp 419–33

Graham, Mrs Maria, *Journal of a Voyage to Brazil and Residence There during Part of the Years 1821, 1822 and 1823* (London, 1824; reprinted New York: F.A. Preager, 1969)

Graham, Mrs Maria, *Journal of a Residence in Chile during the Year 1822* (London, 1824; reprinted New York: F.A. Praeger, 1969)

Graham, R.A. (ed), *The Navy and South America, 1807–1823* (London: Navy Records Society, 1962)

Hall, Captain Basil, *Extracts from a Journal written on the Coasts of Chile, Peru and Mexico, 1820, 1821 and 1822* (Edinburgh: Constable, 1824)

Hall, Captain Basil, *Fragments of Voyages and Travels* (Edinburgh: Cadell, 1832)

Hedderwick, J.B., *The Captain's Clerk* (biography of Thomas Collings, Clerk of the *Owen Glendower*) (London: Hutchinson, 1957)

Hill, Richard, *The Prizes of War* (Stroud: Sutton for RN Museum Publications, 1998)

Humphries, R.A., *British Consular Reports on the Trade and Politics of Latin America* (London: RHS, 1940)

James, E., *Life of Commander Henry James RN* (London: Spottiswood, 1899)

Keppel, Admiral Sir H., *A Sailor's Life under Four Sovereigns* (London: Macmillan, 1899)

Lambert, Andrew, *The Last Sailing Battlefleet* (London: Conway Maritime Press, 1991)

Lavery, Brian, *The Arming and Fitting of English Ships of War, 1600–1815* (London, 1987)

Lavery, Brian, *Nelson's Navy* (London: Conway, 1989)

Lavery, Brian (ed), *Shipboard Life and Organization, 1713–1815* (London: Navy Records Society, 1998)

Lewis, Michael, *The Navy in Transition, A Social History, 1814–1864* (London: Hodder and Stoughton, 1965)

Manrubia, Pilar C, *La Marina de Guerra Española en el Primer Tercio del Siglo XIX* (Madrid: Editorial Naval, 1992)

Marryat, Captain F., *Suggestions for the Abolition of the Present System of Impressment for the Naval Service*, 1822 (extract on the 'Disposition of a Ship's Company', printed in Bromley, J.S. (ed), *The Manning of the Royal Navy* (London: Navy Records Society, 1974))

Morriss, Roger, *Cockburn and the British Navy in Transition* (Exeter: University of Exeter, 1997)

The Navy List, 1819–1829

O'Byrne, William, *Biographical Dictionary* (London: John Murray, 1848), vol 2

Pool, Bernard, *Navy Board Contracts 1660–1832* (London: Longmans, 1966)

Pope, Dudley, *The Black Ship* (London: Weidenfeld and Nicholson, 1963)

Purdy, John, *Description of and Sailing Directions for the Eastern Coast of Brazil* (London: Whittle and Laurie, 1818)

Rodger, N.A.M., *The Wooden World* (London: Fontana, 1986)

Rodger, N.A.M., 'Officers, Gentlemen and Their Education', *Les Empires en Guerre et Paix* (Vincennes, 1990)

Smith, D. Bonner (ed), *Letters of Lord St Vincent* (London: Navy Records Society, 1927), 2 volumes

Vale, Brian, *Independence or Death: British Sailors and Brazilian Independence 1822–25* (London: I.B. Tauris, 1995)

Vale, Brian *'A War Betwixt Englishmen': Brazil versus Argentina in the River Plate, 1825–30* (London: I.B. Tauris, 1999)

Wadia, R.A., *The Bombay Dockyard and the Wadia Master Builders* (Bombay: K.F. Gurd, 1955)

INDEX